OFFICERS and SOLDIERS

CW01020616

THE FRENCH IMPERIAL GUARD 1804-1815

Volume 2
The Cavalry

Part One

André JOUINEAU
Jean-Marie MONGIN

translated from the French by
Alan MCKAY

HISTOIRE & COLLECTIONS

The CAVALRY of the IMPERIAL GUARD

With this second volume of our collection given over to the Imperial Guard, we will be looking at the Cavalry and all mounted troops.

A Herculean task...

As the plates were being made up, we realised that the task was almost impossible: we would be unable to put all the mounted troops into one volume. A third volume and perhaps a fourth will deal with the regiments and other groups which we have been unable to deal with in this second volume.

The richness of the uniforms, the incredible variety of forms of dress worn by the cavalrymen has considerably lengthened the list of the plates which we have to do.

That is why in this volume we have dealt with the first three cavalry corps of the Imperial Guard: *Grenadiers à Cheval, Chasseurs à cheval* (1st and 2nd Regiments) and the Dragoons.

In subsequent volumes we will deal with the Mameluks, the two Chevau-Légers Lancers, the Lithuanian Tartars, the Guards of Honour, and the ephemeral Berg Lancers. Then we shall look at the Gendarmes d'Elite, the Horse Artillery and the other uniforms of the Guard which we have not had space to analyse up to now. So, while waiting, come and discover the sumptuous uniforms of the elite of the *Grande Armée*.

The intelligent arm

For the Emperor, the cavalry was the arm with which he was able to command; it gave him information and enabled him to make his action and his vision felt in the heart and the heat of the engagements.

He had to have as many squadrons as possible to avert danger, to take advantage of the slightest opportunity, and to create an event in the middle of a battle. It was essential for him to have a rapid reaction force of cavalry for manoeuvring (the Light Cavalry), a cavalry unit with which to break up engagements (the Heavy Cavalry) and cavalry for exploiting the terrain (the Cavalry of the Line and the Dragoons). For him, its swiftness made the cavalry the arm of the commander, the weapon par excellence to be used in a crisis.

But if the Emperor wanted his cavalry to be at the forefront, it had to be an intelligent arm, and it was by necessity, then, made up of more highly-qualified officers and more experienced men than the other arms.

Cavalry was the master of movement and was on no account to be mixed up with infantry, where it ran the risk of losing all its capacity to react. Its job was to cover and scout for the infantry not fight by its sides.

This imperial thinking on the subject of the cavalry's role in general was naturally applicable to the cavalry of the Guard which itself, by the very nature of its function as a last resort unit, was the ultimate arm of command, to be used at the height of the engagement.

The great charge made by the Cavalry of the Guard at Austerlitz which broke up the engagement is proof of precisely this.

Cavalry Tactics

The Cavalry of the Guard used the same tactical dispositions as the rest of the cavalry of the Grande Armée.

Established by the Decree of 20 May 1788, then that of *Vendémiaire An XII* (23 September 1804), relating to the manoeuvres of the cavalry when campaigning, the tactics of the cavalry were based above all on the coherence between the four squads in each squadron. There was in effect no real platoon school, nor a school of tactics within the cavalry regiment.

In the same way, as all the men who joined the cavalry regiment could ride a horse, riding lessons were very simple. Emphasis was placed on manoeuvring by squads. The horses that the soldiers had at their disposal in France were very easy to train. Even a rather mediocre rider did not have to worry about his horse-riding ability. Training and experience of battling around together made up the main part of the instruction; hence the great importance given to the older hands in the squadron.

The cavalry marched in columns, four abreast and drew up in columns or in battle formation, always in their squads.

On the battlefield, there were 18 to 20 files (made up of two companies of two squads) on the front. The width of the front expressed in metres was slightly higher than half the strength of the unit committed and deployed.

The charge was carried out at the gallop by staggered squadrons, regiments or brigades.

During battles, these charges were made in columns, so as to take advantage of the spaces between the infantry columns and formations.

These cavalry columns were preceded by tirailleurs whose job it was to scout out the terrain and harass the enemy. It was on this occasion that the musket was most frequently used. The sabre, the lance and the pistols were as a general rule used in charges.

The organisation of the Cavalry

Each unit's history will now be dealt with. We will start with the Cavalry of the Guard's organisation and to some of the more important moments in the Imperial Guard's history.

1804

The *Grenadiers à cheval*, four two-company squadrons (1 018 men and officers)

The *Chasseurs à Cheval* four two- company squadrons.

The *Mameluks*, a company attached to the *Chasseurs à Cheval* (123 cavalrymen and officers).

1806

The *Grenadiers à cheval*, four squadrons of the Old Guard and two squadrons of Velites.

The *Dragoons of the Guard*, two two-company squadrons (832 cavalrymen, Velites and officers).

The *Chasseurs à Cheval*, four squadrons of the Old Guard and two squadrons of Velites.

The *Mameluks* attached to the *Chasseurs à Cheval*, one company (160 men and officers)

1812

The *Grenadiers à cheval*, five two-company squadrons.

The *Dragoons of the Guard*, five two-company squadrons (1 066 Dragoons and officers)

The *Chasseurs à Cheval*, five two-company squadrons.

The *Mameluks*, attached to the *Chasseurs à Cheval* (160 cavalrymen and officers).

1st Regiment of Chevau-Léger Lancers, five two-company squadrons.

2nd Regiment of Chevau-Léger Lancers, five two-company squadrons (1 406 lancers, Velites and officers).

1813

The *Grenadiers à cheval*, four two-company squadrons, then six of which two squadrons of Velites.

The *Dragoons of the Guard*, six two-company squadrons (1 628 men and officers, theoretically)

The *Chasseurs à Cheval*, eight two-company squadrons of which three from the so-called Young Guard.

The *Mameluks*, attached to the Chasseurs à Cheval, one squadron which became momentarily the 10th Squadron of Chasseurs à Cheval.

1st Regiment of Chevau-Léger Lancers, six then nine and finally ten squadrons with two companies. One company of lancer-scouts was attached to the regiment.

2nd Regiment of Chevau-Léger Lancers, eight two-squadron companies (2 000 men theoretically).

1st Regiment of the Guard of Honour.
2nd Regiment of the Guard of Honour.
3rd Regiment of the Guard of Honour.
4th Regiment of the Guard of Honour.

1815.

The *Grenadiers à cheval*, four two-company squadrons (1 042 men and officers)

The *Dragoons of the Guard*, four two-company squadrons (1 026 men and officers theoretically).

The *Chasseurs à Cheval*, four two-company squadrons.

The *2nd Regiment of Chasseurs à Cheval.*

The *Mameluks*, one two-company squadron.

A Regiment of Chevau-Légers of the Imperial Guard, four squadrons, two companies strong (one company of Polish Lancers returning from Elba, amalgamated with the other lancers from the regiment which existed before the first abdication).

Pictures from legend...

From the victorious charge of the Grenadiers and the *Chasseurs à Cheval* at Marengo, to the terrible charge of the Lancers at Waterloo, the death of Morland at the head of the *Chasseurs* and the *Mameluks* at Austerlitz, the history of the cavalry of the Guard is full of glorious feats of arms, on a par with the magnificence of its uniforms.

The GRENADIERS A CHEVAL

From one set of regulations to another, in bad circumstances as well as good, the organisation of the — which are considered traditionally as the first and foremost of the cavalry regiments of the *'Vieille Garde'* (the Old Guard) — developed rather less chaotically than others in this famous unit.

One could say that the birth of the Imperial Guard goes back to the amalgamation of the *'Garde du Directoire'* (a unit which was very demanding when it came to recruitment) and the *'Garde du Corps Législatif'*. The ebullient General Murat commanded this new *'Garde des Consuls'* (Consular Guard). On 3 January 1800, Brigade Commander Bessières organised the cavalry in this new unit.

The Grenadiers à cheval (*The Horse Grenadiers*)

The Horse Grenadiers of the Consular Guard were first of all organised into two squadrons in 1800 and then increased to three on 10 October 1801. On 14 November of the same year, the three squadrons became five. Brigade Commander's cavalrymen took on the name of *Régiment des grenadiers à cheval de la Garde impériale* (the Imperial Guard's Horse Grenadier Regiment) definitively on 18 May 1804.

The two squadrons of the Consular Guard of 1800 ran to 226 cavalrymen and eight officers whereas the four squadrons of 1802 had 41 officers and 960 Grenadiers à cheval. The cavalry regiment on its creation had four squadrons of two companies, for a theoretical total strength of 1 018 men. On 30 *Fructidor An XIII* (17 September 1805), they were joined by a first squadron of Velites and then a second. In 1811, with the disappearance of the two squadrons of Velites, the regiment grew to five battle squadrons. Upon the return from Russia, in 1813, as the regiment only had a few more than 120 cavalrymen on the rolls, the Guard's administration reduced the number of squadrons back to four. The Imperial decree dated 10 January 1813 granted the regiment one, then two Velites squadrons which were called the Young Guard.

The *Grenadiers à cheval* of the Guard were disbanded on 23 July 1814 only to be recreated on 8 April 1815 before disappearing for good on 25 November of the same year.

During the first Restoration, the regiment was used to re-structure the *'Corps Royal des Cuirassiers de France'* (France's Royal Corps of Cuirassiers). This unit was made up of four squadrons with a total of 63 officers and 979 men.

It was with this organisation that the regiment went to Belgium alongside the other units of the Imperial Guard.

The Velites

The Velites were considered as reinforcements for the battle squadrons used to make up the losses as and when necessary in the companies. They were young recruits who did not necessarily come from other units in the French Army. They were required to measure the right size like their elders, to pay for their uniforms and to be able to show an annual income of at least 300 Francs.

The aim was to recruit among the sons of the Empire's lower bourgeoisie, which Napoleon was trying to flatter and win over to him by allowing their sons to get into the Army Corps' most glorious unit.

Music in the Grenadiers à cheval

One cannot really speak of music in the cavalry as one could in the infantry. In fact, music in the Grenadiers à cheval was restricted to trumpeters and kettledrummers, to which were added the drums of the foot service for the period 1808-1811.

There were three trumpeters per company (6 per squadron) therefore 24 for a four-squadron regiment together with a trumpet major and two trumpeters with headquarters, to which a twenty-eighth musician had to be added, the timpanist or kettledrummer.

In 1813, after the terrible Russian Campaign, it seems that the timpanist had disappeared from the regiment.

During their short existence, the Horse Grenadier drummers numbered eight commanded by a drummaster.

The Horse Grenadier timpanist was enrolled in 1802 with the rank of 'brigadier-trompette-timbalier' and disappeared in the turmoil of the retreat from Russia. Note that during march pasts the timpanist wearing their hussar-like full-dress, led the parade in front of the regimental trumpeters.

The problem of ranks in the Guard

The Horse Grenadier ranks were those in use in the cavalry of the line, though this has to be explained further. Indeed, the Emperor established the principle of assimilation on 19 March 1803, whereby a cavalryman whith, for example, the rank of leutnant in the Guard transferred to the Line with a higher rank, i.e. captain. Thus a major in the Guard had the rank of colonel in the cavalry of the line (see table below).

In the Guard, the marks of rank were the same physically as the Line. But there was more than that to the principle of assimilation. A squadron commander in the Guards Grenadiers à cheval transferring to the cavalry of the Line would automatically take the rank of Major, unless he had served for four years in the Guard in that capacity (Squadron Commander was therefore equivalent to major), in which case he would be made colonel in the cavalry of the Line.

A few famous names...

In 1806, Maréchal Bessières had been *Colonel-General* of the Guard Cavalry since 1804.

Major-General Walther commanded the *Grenadiers à cheval*, Colonel Baron Lepic was a *major* (lieutenant-colonel) in the regiment, Colonel Chastel was *major en second* (second lieutenant-colonel).

In 1813, Maréchal Suchet was *Colonel-General* of the Cavalry of the Guards cavalry; he was appointed six months after the death of Bessières. Major-General Walther still commanded the regiment, Brigadier Lafférière-Lévèque was *major* whereas Baron Castex also a Brigadier, was *major en second* (second lieutenant-colonel).

THE GUARD AND LINE EQUIVALENTS

GUARD	LINE	GUARD	LINE
Soldier	Corporal	2nd Lieutenant	Lieutenant
Corporal	Sergeant	1st Lieutenant	Captain
Sergeant	*Adjudant sous-officier*	Captain	Battalion Cdr
		Battalion Cdr	Major
Sergeant-Major	Second -lieutenant	Major	Colonel

CAVALRY AND INFANTRY EQUIVALENTS

CAVALRY	INFANTRY
Brigadier	Corporal
Maréchal-des-logis	Sergeant
Maréchal des-logis-chef	Sergeant-Major
Chef d'escadrons	Battalion Commander (Major)

The rank of Fourrier *(Quartermaster) was the equivalent of Maréchal-des-Logis*

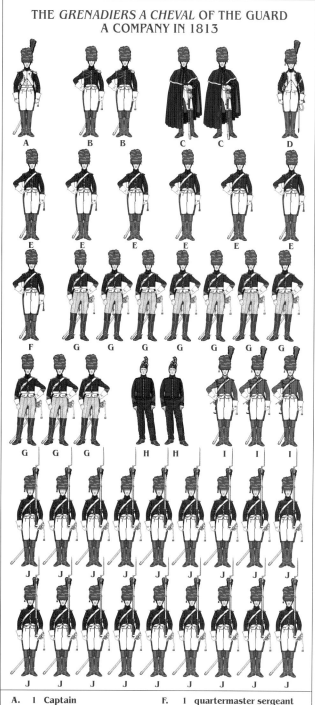

THE *GRENADIERS A CHEVAL* OF THE GUARD
A COMPANY IN 1813

A.	1	Captain	F.	1	quartermaster sergeant
B.	2	First lieutenants	G.	10	corporals (*brigadiers*)
C.	2	Second lieutenants	H.	2	blacksmiths
D.	1	*maréchal-des-logis-chef*	I.	3	trumpeters
E.	6	*maréchaux-des-logis*	J.	96	Cavalrymen

FULL DRESS

Cavalryman in full dress for duty on foot around 1808. The sabre was carried saltire-wise, the belt was worn like an infantry light sabre strap.

Brigadier in full dress. At the beginning of the Empire, the grenadiers wore golden-yellow trefoil epaulettes. Like the foot grenadiers they wore a pair of golden ear-rings. Their hair was powdered, plaited and worn in a pony-tail.

The *Grenadiers à cheval* of the Guard were not forgotten when it came to them being given nicknames by their brothers-in-arms in the infantry of the Guard or other units in the cavalry of the Line.
Where the Cuirassiers, the epitome of the heavy cavalry, were called the *'Gros Frères'* (big brothers) by the other soldiers in the Grande Armée, the Grenadiers à cheval were given the name *'Gros Talons'* (big heels).

Cavalryman in full dress around 1808. In this dress, the grenadiers wore strong boots with smooth one-piece legs.

Cavalryman in full dress for duty on foot around 1808. The first ring of the sabre has been hung on the hook (used for just this purpose) on the belt so that it can be worn in this manner.

TOWN and QUARTER DRESS

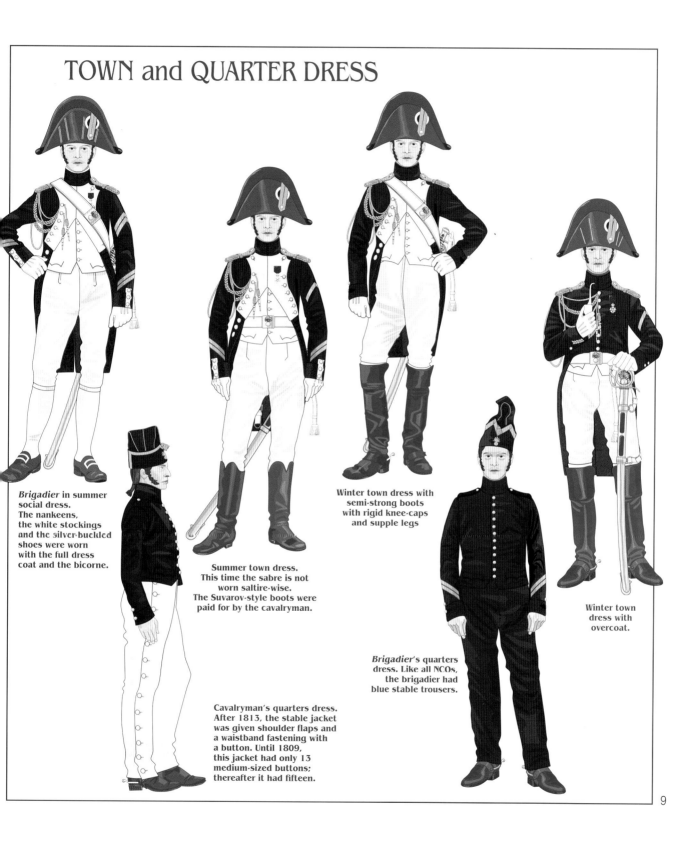

Brigadier in summer social dress. The nankeens, the white stockings and the silver-buckled shoes were worn with the full dress coat and the bicorne.

Summer town dress. This time the sabre is not worn saltire-wise. The Suvarov-style boots were paid for by the cavalryman.

Cavalryman's quarters dress. After 1813, the stable jacket was given shoulder flaps and a waistband fastening with a button. Until 1809, this jacket had only 13 medium-sized buttons; thereafter it had fifteen.

Winter town dress with semi-strong boots with rigid knee-caps and supple legs

Brigadier's quarters dress. Like all NCOs, the brigadier had blue stable trousers.

Winter town dress with overcoat.

The GRENADIER in CAMPAIGN DRESS

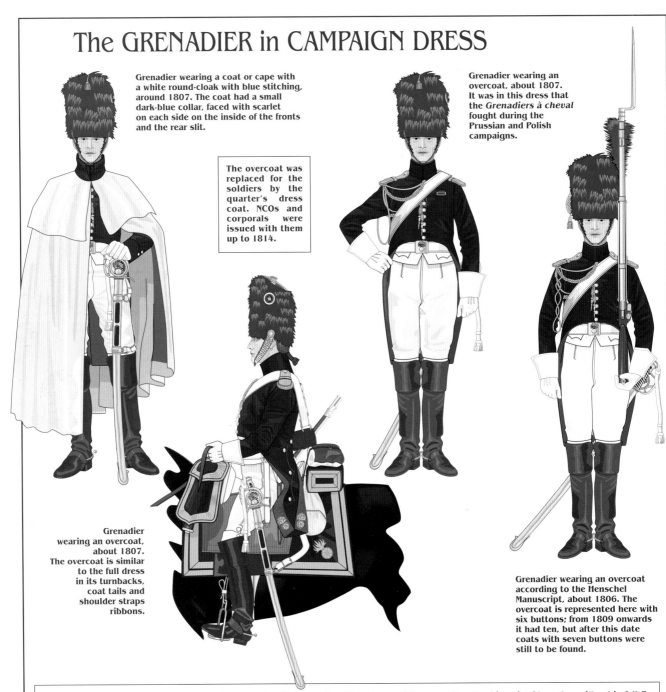

Grenadier wearing a coat or cape with a white round-cloak with blue stitching, around 1807. The coat had a small dark-blue collar, faced with scarlet on each side on the inside of the fronts and the rear slit.

The overcoat was replaced for the soldiers by the quarter's dress coat. NCOs and corporals were issued with them up to 1814.

Grenadier wearing an overcoat, about 1807. It was in this dress that the *Grenadiers à cheval* fought during the Prussian and Polish campaigns.

Grenadier wearing an overcoat, about 1807. The overcoat is similar to the full dress in its turnbacks, coat tails and shoulder straps ribbons.

Grenadier wearing an overcoat according to the Henschel Manuscript, about 1806. The overcoat is represented here with six buttons; from 1809 onwards it had ten, but after this date coats with seven buttons were still to be found.

Until 1813, the grenadier's wardrobe consisted of four different pairs of breeches and trousers. One doeskin pair of breeches with a big fall fly was used by the cavalrymen in full dress; a second -sheepskin- pair was worn for ordinary dress. While campaigning, and for marches, the cavalryman wore a pair of twill over-trousers which fastened on each side with 16 little bone buttons. A pair of white canvas trousers, worn as stable dress and fastening along the whole length of the leg with 18 bone buttons, completed the wardrobe.
It was only in 1813 that the first horse-riding trousers in grey cloth appeared. The area between the legs was protected by an extra piece of cloth to reinforce it. Moreover, two square patches on the thighs protected them from the rubbing of the sabre and the rifle.

MARCHING and CAMPAIGN DRESS

Cavalryman from one of the two squadrons of Velites, from the so-called Young Guard, created in January 1813. He is wearing the same uniform as the Old Guard cavalryman but without the aglet. Moreover the equipment made with buffalo-hide does not have any stitching. He is not wearing ear-rings and his hair is short.

Brigadier in campaign dress about 1810. The overcoat has been replaced by a second uniform coat with lapels and square facings at the bottom of the coat. The quality of the cloth was not so good.

On campaign, the *Grenadiers à cheval* wore semi-strong boots with rigid knee-caps and supple legs. On certain battlefields, they sometimes wore the stiff-legged full dress boots (see page 8).

Cavalryman wearing campaign dress about 1810. He is wearing the second uniform coat with twill over-trousers fastening on the sides by means of sixteen bone buttons. The water bottle is an hollowed-out colocynth.

Grenadier wearing a hooded coat brought into service in 1813. It had sleeves and six golden-yellow woollen open-work coil frogs. Three big uniform buttons fastened the collar.

Grenadier wearing campaign dress, about 1813. The grey cloth riding breeches came into service that year.

11

CAMPAIGN DRESS in BELGIUM, 1815

After the Emperor's abdication in 1814, the *Grenadiers à cheval* became the *Corps Royal des cuirassiers de France*. Cuirassier jacket were made up whilst waiting for the breast-plates and the helmets. However, the political events overtook the establishment of the new cuirassier corps, and the grenadiers returned to the Imperial Guard with this uniform. The trumpeter, wearing a dark-blue coat with the King's livery, very quickly reverted to his Guard's uniform during the Hundred Days.

Equipment, armament and harnesses remained the same. The imperial marks were most probably put back on the bearskins though not necessarily in all cases.

Horse grenadier in campaign dress, June 1815. The jacket-coat worn by this cavalryman is indeed that designed for the cuirassiers and not a overcoat with shortened skirts. This uniform was less spruce than the coat, even of the second uniform but it was more practical for fighting.

The strength of the Regiment in 1813. There were a headquarters and six squadrons of Grenadiers à cheval of whom two were from the Young Guard (the 5th and 6th Squadrons), with 91 officers and 1 540 men.

Headquarters was made up of:
1 Colonel (in fact a Major-General)
2 Majors
1 Squadron Commander Instructor
3 Adjudant-Captains (Administration)
4 *Sous-Adjudants Majors*
4 Eagle Bearers
3 Surgeon-Majors
3 Assistant Surgeon-Majors
1 Under-Instructor
1 Quartermaster
2 Veterinaries (Surgeons)
4 Assistant veterinaries
1 Trumpet-Major
2 *Brigadiers-Trompettes*

6 Master-craftsmen
2 Master-Blacksmiths

At this period each company was made up of:
1 Captain
2 First-Lieutenants
2 Second-Lieutenants
1 *Maréchal-des-Logis-Chef*
6 *Maréchal-des-Logis*
1 Quartermaster
10 *Brigadiers*
2 Blacksmiths
3 Trumpeters
96 *Grenadiers à cheval*

In 1814, the *Corps des Cuirassiers de France* consisted of four squadrons, with 63 officers and 979 men. It was thus that the recently re-created Horse Grenadier Regiment of the Imperial Guard went off to Belgium in June 1815.

CLOTHING

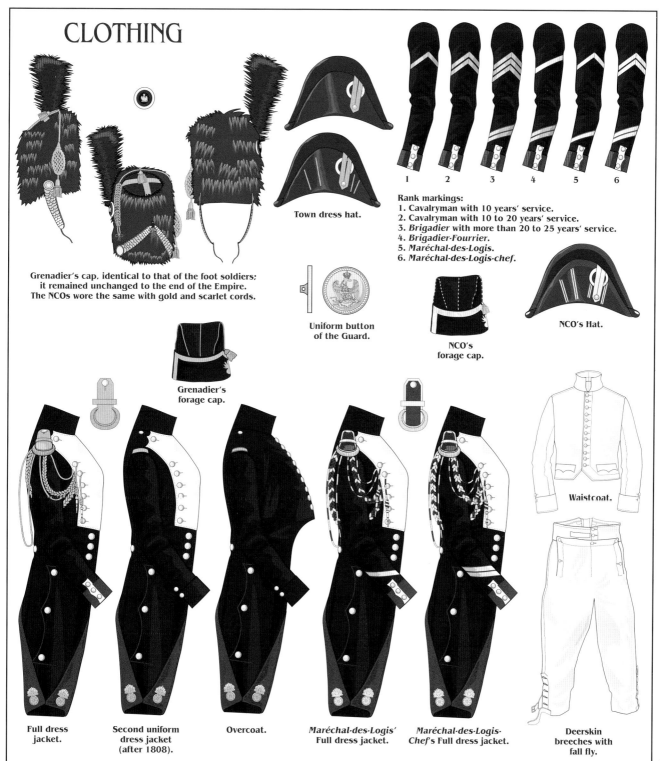

Grenadier's cap, identical to that of the foot soldiers;
it remained unchanged to the end of the Empire.
The NCOs wore the same with gold and scarlet cords.

Town dress hat.

Rank markings:
1. Cavalryman with 10 years' service.
2. Cavalryman with 10 to 20 years' service.
3. *Brigadier* with more than 20 to 25 years' service.
4. *Brigadier-Fourrier.*
5. *Maréchal-des-Logis.*
6. *Maréchal-des-Logis-chef.*

Uniform button
of the Guard.

NCO's
forage cap.

NCO's Hat.

Grenadier's
forage cap.

Waistcoat.

Full dress
jacket.

Second uniform
dress jacket
(after 1808).

Overcoat.

Maréchal-des-Logis'
Full dress jacket.

*Maréchal-des-Logis-
Chef's* Full dress jacket.

Deerskin
breeches with
fall fly.

13

ARMAMENT and EQUIPMENT

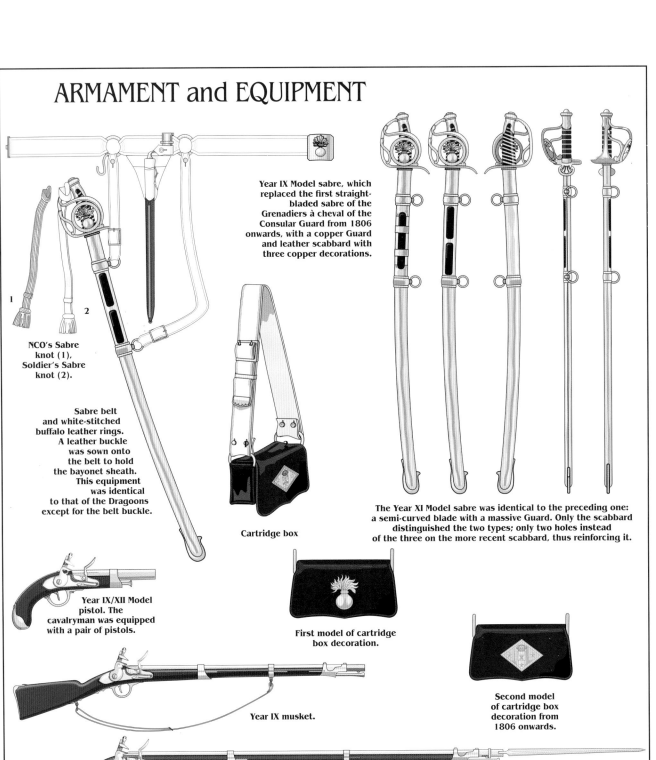

NCO's Sabre knot (1), Soldier's Sabre knot (2).

Sabre belt and white-stitched buffalo leather rings. A leather buckle was sown onto the belt to hold the bayonet sheath. This equipment was identical to that of the Dragoons except for the belt buckle.

Year IX/XII Model pistol. The cavalryman was equipped with a pair of pistols.

Cartridge box

Year IX Model sabre, which replaced the first straight-bladed sabre of the Grenadiers à cheval of the Consular Guard from 1806 onwards, with a copper Guard and leather scabbard with three copper decorations.

The Year XI Model sabre was identical to the preceding one: a semi-curved blade with a massive Guard. Only the scabbard distinguished the two types; only two holes instead of the three on the more recent scabbard, thus reinforcing it.

First model of cartridge box decoration.

Second model of cartridge box decoration from 1806 onwards.

Year IX musket.

Infantry rifle of the Guard and its bayonet distributed to the Velites then to the Grenadiers from 1806 onwards.

SADDLES

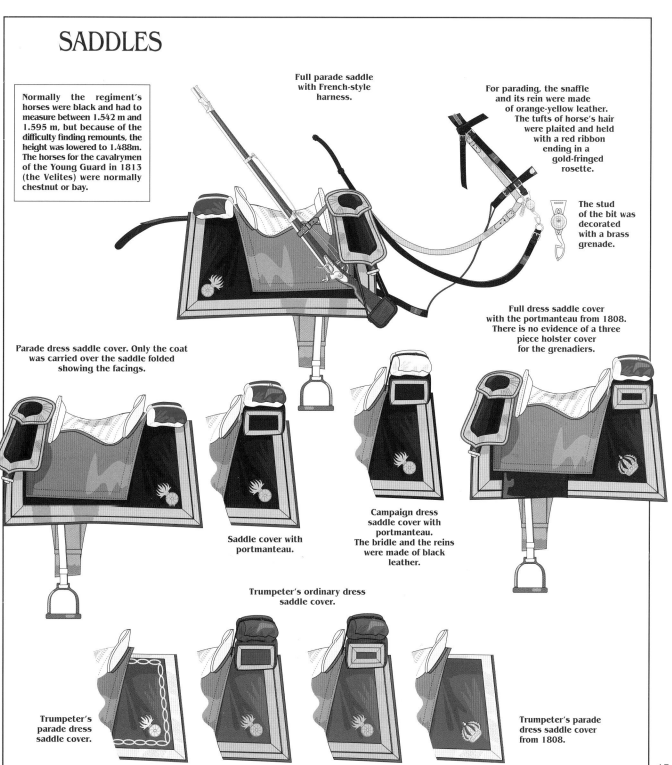

Normally the regiment's horses were black and had to measure between 1.542 m and 1.595 m, but because of the difficulty finding remounts, the height was lowered to 1.488m. The horses for the cavalrymen of the Young Guard in 1813 (the Velites) were normally chestnut or bay.

Full parade saddle with French-style harness.

For parading, the snaffle and its rein were made of orange-yellow leather. The tufts of horse's hair were plaited and held with a red ribbon ending in a gold-fringed rosette.

The stud of the bit was decorated with a brass grenade.

Parade dress saddle cover. Only the coat was carried over the saddle folded showing the facings.

Full dress saddle cover with the portmanteau from 1808. There is no evidence of a three piece holster cover for the grenadiers.

Saddle cover with portmanteau.

Campaign dress saddle cover with portmanteau. The bridle and the reins were made of black leather.

Trumpeter's ordinary dress saddle cover.

Trumpeter's parade dress saddle cover.

Trumpeter's parade dress saddle cover from 1808.

15

The NCOs

Maréchal-des-Logis-Chef wearing a frock coat. *The Maréchal-des-Logis-Chef* 's aglets were mixed, two thirds and one third for the Maréchal-des-Logis and the quartermasters.

Maréchal-des-Logis in stable dress.

Maréchal-des-Logis wearing an overcoat.

Maréchal-des-Logis in full dress.

Maréchal-des-Logis during the Belgian campaign in 1815.

Maréchal-des-Logis in service full dress about 1810.

Maréchal-des-Logis wearing a cape.

16

The TRUMPETERS

Trumpeter in parade dress towards 1806. Traditionally, cavalry trumpeters mounted a grey or white horse.

Brigadier-Trompette in parade dress towards 1808.

Trumpet-Major in parade dress towards 1810. The new model of hat must have been of the same quality as those of senior officers.

The full uniform which was rarely worn by the trumpeters of the *Grenadiers à cheval* of the Guard, was made up of the sky-blue jacket with a collar of the same colour. The lapels, the facings and the straps were made of scarlet cloth. The long pockets were simulated by scarlet piping. The turn backs were made of scarlet serge. The flat buttons were made of gold-covered copper. A gold stripe edged the collar, the lapels, the facings and the pockets. It also surrounded the waist buttons and the six button-holes on each lapel. All the button holes were finished with a twisted fringe which the inventories called frogs (*brandenbourgs*). The ornaments of the turn backs were gold grenades.

The TRUMPETERS

Trumpeter in full service dress towards 1808. In this dress as with the campaign dress, the trumpeters wore the grenadiers' bearskin.

Trumpeter wearing an overcoat.

Trumpeter wearing stable dress. The clothing was identical with that of the other grenadiers, only the colour of the bottom of the jacket was different.

Trumpeter wearing a coat. There is no evidence of a coat with a hood at the end of the Empire.

Trumpeter on horseback wearing an overcoat.

Trumpeter in campaign dress towards 1810, wearing the jacket of the second uniform.

Trumpeter in town dress towards 1806.

Trumpeter according to the 'Otto Manuscript' towards 1807.

Drummer towards 1808 for foot duty.

Trumpeters in town dress wearing the jacket and the overcoat.

Trumpeter-pupil. He only wore an overcoat without any rank stripes but with the aglets. The forage cap was the only head-dress permitted.

19

CLOTHING

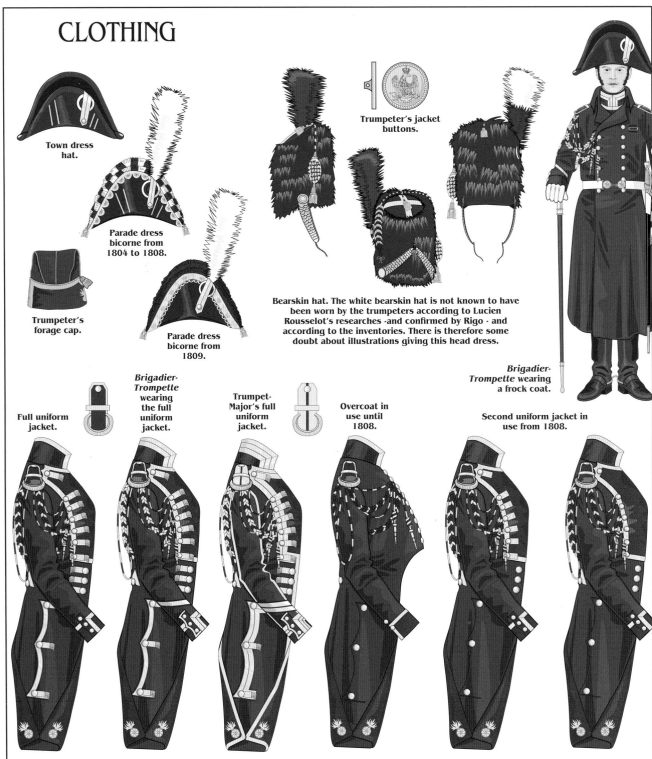

Town dress hat.

Parade dress bicorne from 1804 to 1808.

Trumpeter's forage cap.

Parade dress bicorne from 1809.

Trumpeter's jacket buttons.

Bearskin hat. The white bearskin hat is not known to have been worn by the trumpeters according to Lucien Rousselot's researches -and confirmed by Rigo - and according to the inventories. There is therefore some doubt about illustrations giving this head dress.

Brigadier-Trompette wearing a frock coat.

Full uniform jacket.

Brigadier-Trompette wearing the full uniform jacket.

Trumpet-Major's full uniform jacket.

Overcoat in use until 1808.

Second uniform jacket in use from 1808.

The KETTLEDRUMMER

The kettledrummer in the *Grenadiers à cheval* is known through the drawings of Hoffmann, which were taken up by Lucien Rousselot and Rigo in the plate *'Le Plumet'* No 5. According to different interpretations, he may vary in certain details of equipment and embroidery. In 1811, the kettledrummer received a new scarlet dolman with blue facings decorated with gold stripes. It cannot be confirmed that the kettledrummer kept his splendid scarlet pelisse. The kettledrummer in the Grenadiers à cheval unlike his opposite number in the Chasseurs was a mature man, wearing whiskers in the original picture.

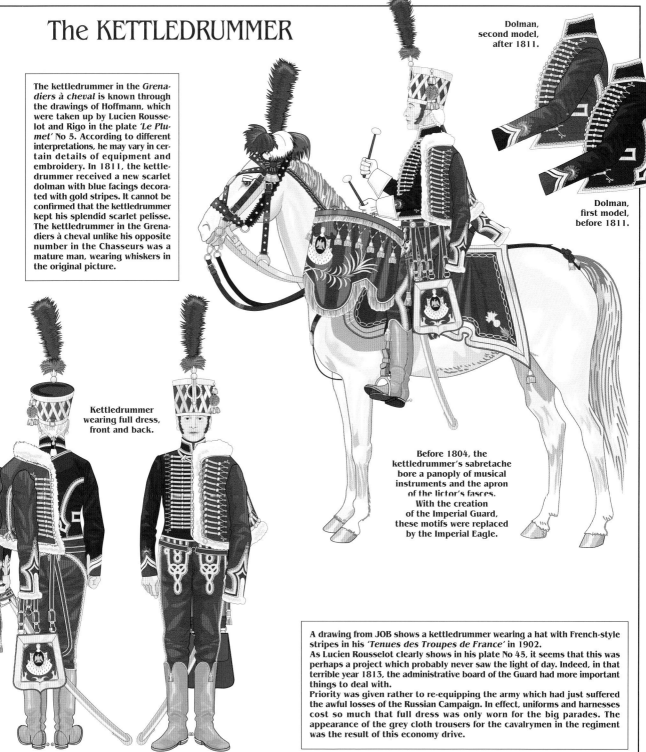

Dolman, second model, after 1811.

Dolman, first model, before 1811.

Kettledrummer wearing full dress, front and back.

Before 1804, the kettledrummer's sabretache bore a panoply of musical instruments and the apron of the lictor's fasces. With the creation of the Imperial Guard, these motifs were replaced by the Imperial Eagle.

A drawing from JOB shows a kettledrummer wearing a hat with French-style stripes in his *'Tenues des Troupes de France'* in 1902.
As Lucien Rousselot clearly shows in his plate No 45, it seems that this was perhaps a project which probably never saw the light of day. Indeed, in that terrible year 1813, the administrative board of the Guard had more important things to deal with.
Priority was given rather to re-equipping the army which had just suffered the awful losses of the Russian Campaign. In effect, uniforms and harnesses cost so much that full dress was only worn for the big parades. The appearance of the grey cloth trousers for the cavalrymen in the regiment was the result of this economy drive.

21

The OFFICERS

Officer in full
service dress.

Officer
in Campaign
dress.

Officer
in Quarters
dress.

Officer
in social
dress.

Senior Officer.
They were the only ones
to own a saddle which had
three-piece flaps.
For parading, the officers
could wear an even
more richly decorated
sword, made by Boutet.

Officer wearing
a coat with
the big stripe
on the collar.

Officer
wearing
an overcoat.

STANDARDS

The Eagle in 1804.

Standard-Bearer towards 1808. He is wearing the regimental headquarters white plume.

Reverse of the model 1804 standard.

L'EMPEREUR
DES FRANCAIS,
AU RÉG.ᵗ DE GRENADIERS
À CHEVAL
DE LA GARDE
IMPÉRIALE

Obverse of the model 1804 standard.

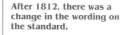

After 1812, there was a change in the wording on the standard.

L'EMPEREUR
DES FRANÇAIS
AU RÉGᵐᵗ DE GRENADIERS
A CHEVAL
DE LA GARDE
IMPÉRIALE

became

GARDE IMPÉRIALE
L'EMPEREUR NAPOLÉON
AU RÉGIMENT
DES GRENADIERS
A CHEVAL

The Eagles were carried during the 1805, 1806 and 1807 campaigns. When they returned to Paris, the town presented them with gold crowns.

Model 1812 standard. It bears the same names of battles as that of the Foot Grenadier regiment.

The originals were destroyed during the first abdication.

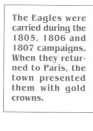

Standard-Bearer towards 1805. Note the standard-bearer's banderole.

ILLUSTRATED GLOSSARY

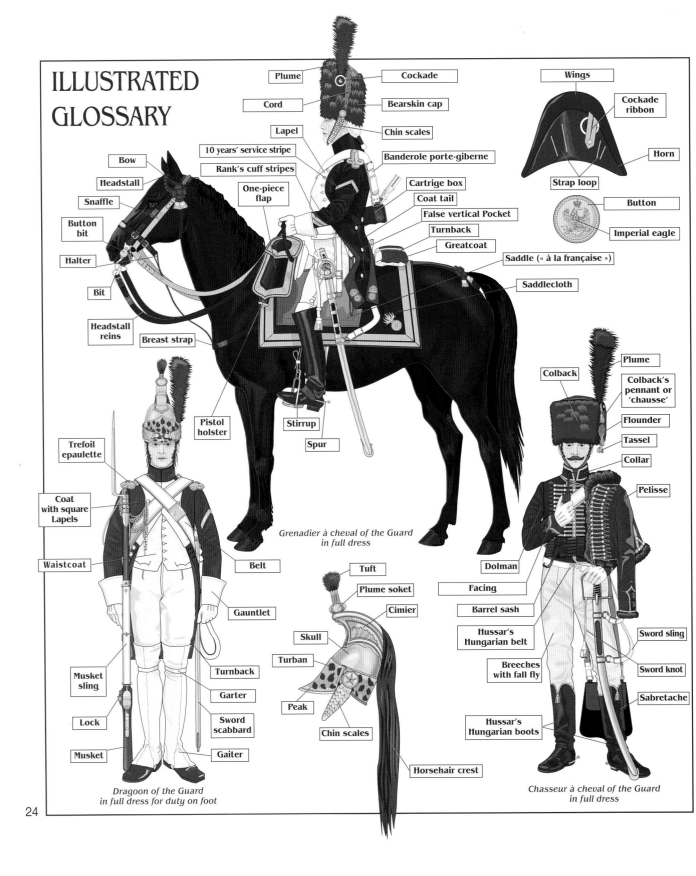

Plume
Cockade
Cord
Bearskin cap
Lapel
Chin scales
10 years' service stripe
Banderole porte-giberne
Rank's cuff stripes
Cartrige box
One-piece flap
Coat tail
False vertical Pocket
Turnback
Greatcoat
Saddle (« à la française »)
Saddlecloth

Wings
Cockade ribbon
Horn
Strap loop
Button
Imperial eagle

Bow
Headstall
Snaffle
Button bit
Halter
Bit
Headstall reins
Breast strap
Pistol holster
Stirrup
Spur

Grenadier à cheval of the Guard in full dress

Trefoil epaulette
Coat with square Lapels
Waistcoat
Belt
Gauntlet
Musket sling
Turnback
Garter
Lock
Sword scabbard
Musket
Gaiter

Dragoon of the Guard in full dress for duty on foot

Tuft
Plume soket
Cimier
Skull
Turban
Peak
Chin scales
Horsehair crest

Colback
Plume
Colback's pennant or 'chausse'
Flounder
Tassel
Collar
Pelisse
Dolman
Facing
Barrel sash
Hussar's Hungarian belt
Breeches with fall fly
Sword sling
Sword knot
Sabretache
Hussar's Hungarian boots

Chasseur à cheval of the Guard in full dress

24

The DRAGOONS in the IMPERIAL GUARD

The Imperial Decree of 15 April 1806 ordered the creation of the Regiment of Dragoons of the Imperial Guard. It was about time! Ever since the creation of the regiment under the *Ancien Régime* the Dragoons had never had the privilege of serving the monarch so closely.

It goes without saying that the behaviour of the Dragoons of the Line during the recent campaigns had gone a long way to helping the Emperor to take this decision.

The regiment was first made up of two squadrons, then a third of Velites was added before the whole went up to four squadrons of old hands and one of Velites. On 1 January 1812, during one of the re-organisations of the Imperial Guard, the squadron of Velites was disbanded and the regiment then numbered five squadrons of Dragoons. From 1813 to 1814, like the regiment of Grenadiers à cheval of the Guard, the regiment of Dragoons numbered six squadrons of which two in the Young Guard. On 12 May 1814, Louis XVIII changed the regiment to the *Corps Royal des dragons de France* with four squadrons. The Hundred Days saw the regiment reborn under the title of Dragoons of the Imperial Guard, still with four squadrons. The regiment was finally disbanded during the winter of 1815.

When the Dragoons of the Guard were created, each regiment of Dragoons of the Line had to supply twelve men having ten years' service and measuring at least 1 metre 73 cms. These indications saved the regiments of the Line being bled of their oldest veterans but did not make the creation of the new regiment any easier.

Indeed on 11 September 1806, almost five months after the creation of the regiment, the first two squadrons were scarcely up to full strength. It would only be 1807 when the number of cavalrymen went beyond the five hundred mark, including officers (608 cavalrymen and 48 officers).

In 1812 for the great Russian Campaign, the regiment numbered 1 088 men and 64 officers divided among five squadrons. Only 130 Dragoons came back from the steppes of Russia among whom 11 officers.

The six squadrons of the 1813 re-organisation numbered 1 537 men and 91 officers, whereas the *Corps Royal des Dragons de France* only had 592 men and 42 officers. The Emperor was able to put 53 officers and 973 men into the Belgian Campaign. The King sacked the surviving 30 officers and 641 men in the winter of 1815.

The Velites

Like the *Chasseurs à Cheval* or the *Grenadiers à cheval* of the Guard, the Velites in the Dragoons were recruited among the sons from good families who could own to an annual income of at least 300 francs, could buy their own uniform, could read and write and were of the required height.

When the regiment went off campaigning, the Velites were divided among the battle companies. One of the peculiarities of the Velites wasthe possibility for them, at the end of three years' service, to join one of the Old Guards' regiment or be appointed NCO in another regiment of the line. Some, among the best, could even be directly promoted to officer rank in a regiment of the line. For example, in 1811 when the Velites squadron was disbanded, the cavalrymen were placed in the first four regiments of the Line, made up the backbone of the fifth squadron or were split among the other regiments of the Line.

A few famous names...

First of all, Joséphine de Beauharnais who was the regiment's Godmother and gave the Dragoons of the Guard their nickname of *'the Empress' Dragoons'*. In 1806, the regiment was commanded by Arrighi de Casanova, the former commander of the corps of the 1st Regiment of Dragoons. He had under his command Squadron Commanders Fitteau, Lefort, Jolivet and Rossignol. In 1809, the Dragoons were under the command of Major-General Bonardi de Saint-Sulpice. In 1813, Count Ornano, a Major-General, was *Colonel-Commandant* of the regiment. Brigadier Count Letort was *Major* with Colonel Pinteville *Major en second* (second Lieutenant-colonel). Letort was *Colonel-Commandant* of the regiment at Waterloo where he was killed.

Old or Young Guard?

For the cavalry the following were considered as being **Old Guard:** the cavalrymen and NCOs of the regiments or squadrons from the *Grenadiers à cheval*, the *Chasseurs à Cheval*, Dragoon cavalrymen and NCOs of the 1st Regiment of Chevau-Légers Lancers, the Mameluks.

In the **Middle Guard**: the NCOs and soldiers of the 2nd Regiment of Chevau-Légers Lancers.

In the **Young Guard**: the squadrons of the regiments of Old Guard created in 1813.

DRAGON FULL DRESS

Cavalryman in full service dress on foot towards 1808. The sabre was worn saltire-wise with the belt worn like an Infantry light sabre strap.

Brigadier's full dress. Unlike the grenadiers, the Dragoons wore their hair short, 'Titus'-style, and wore no ear-rings. The jacket was identical with that of the grenadiers but was 'Dragoon' green. The saddle cover had the smallest stripe on the inside and the piping was green. Dragoons mounted bays.

Cavalryman wearing full dress around 1807, seen from the right.

Cavalryman in full service dress around 1808. The first ring of the sabre has been hung on the hook (intended for just this purpose) on the belt so that it can be worn in this manner, which was common to the Grenadiers and Dragoons.

DRAGON FULL DRESS

Velite in full service dress towards 1808. These were young volunteers whose parents gave them 300 francs every year annually.

Cavalryman in full dress on foot around 1808.
For this full dress there was a pair of white gaiters.

Cavalryman in full parade dress for the wedding of Napoleon and Archduchess Marie-Louise of Austria.

Unlike the Grenadiers à cheval of the Guard, the Dragoons were never issued with the undress jacket.

They were however given, probably from 1808, a second full dress jacket. This enabled them to use the new jacket for full dress and the second more worn jacket for ordinary service or for campaign life.

The overcoat was used, like the Grenadiers, also on campaign during the first years of the regiment's existence.

Unlike the Grenadiers, the Dragoons did not have strong boots with smooth legs, but only semi-rigid boots with knee caps, or 'Suvaroff' -style boots which the Dragoons had to get for themselves individually.

Brigadier in full service dress towards 1811. It was from this time on that the little green triangles disappeared from the bottom of the turn backs sewn on the skirts and that three-piece holster covers started to appear in 1808.

TOWN and QUARTERS DRESS

Winter town dress, according to the set of etchings by Martinet. The shape of the hat corresponded to the fashion of the time. The hussar-style or 'à la Souvarov' boots were at the cavalryman's expense.

Winter town dress, overcoat. The aglets were also worn on the overcoat.

Stable dress. The natural-coloured canvas trousers were fastened with 18 bone buttons on each leg. The stable jacket was green, the Dragoons' green.

Winter Guard dress or sentry-duty dress. According to Lucien Rousselot, this was a coat and hood destined for precisely this use.

The Dragoon used gauntlets with had removable sleevelets. The Dragoons of the Guard also had large-collared coats, or coats with a white round-cloak stitched with blue. The collar was green with red caddis facings placed like those of the Grenadiers à cheval. In 1813, the hooded coat was distributed to the Dragoons. The round-cloak like that of the grenadiers was longer and had six aurora woollen frogs which ended in a tuft. The buttons were on the right and the holes on the left.

Summer town dress, according to Lucien Rousselot's set of plates of the French Army.

MARCHING and CAMPAIGN DRESS

Campaign dress, overcoat, 1806-1810. This was the main item in the campaign dress kit, the full dress jacket being left behind at the dépôt.

Campaign dress with overcoat towards 1810 after a German etching showing scarlet piping which had no *raison d'être*.

Campaign dress, overcoat, 1806-1810.
In 1812, the Dragoons left with their worn full dress uniform.

As well as their wide deerskin breeches protected from rubbing by cloth knee pads, the Dragoons had twill over-trousers from the creation of the regiment. Riding breeches reinforced with grey cloth arrived in the corps to replace the old ones in 1811.
Nankeen trousers and the stable trousers completed the Dragoon's kit.

A coat with a round-cloak, first model, without the scarlet caddis sleeves.

The second model of the coat with the round-cloak with sleeves used at the end of the Empire from 1813.

CAMPAIGN DRESS

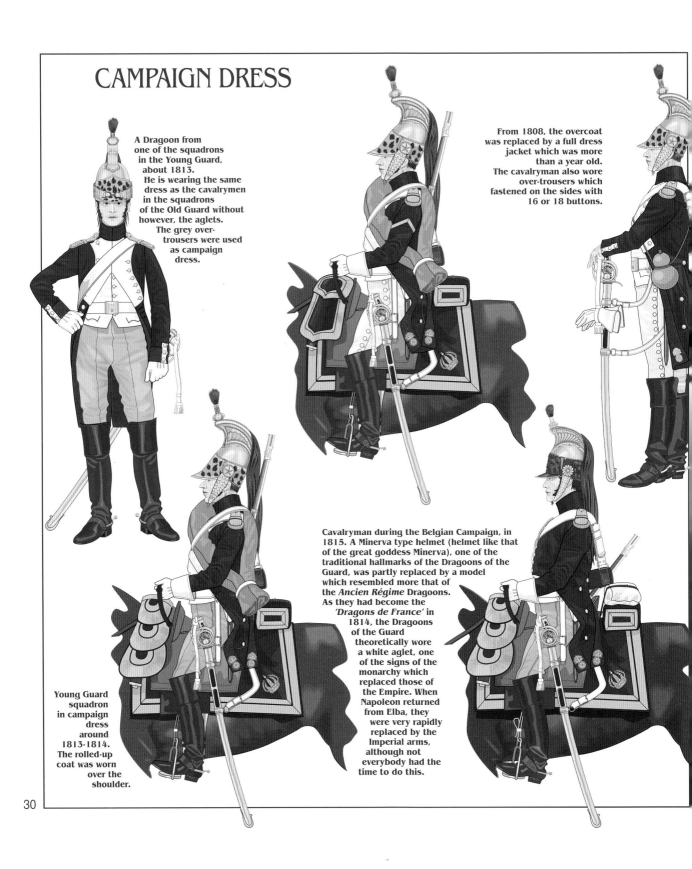

A Dragoon from one of the squadrons in the Young Guard, about 1813. He is wearing the same dress as the cavalrymen in the squadrons of the Old Guard without however, the aglets. The grey over-trousers were used as campaign dress.

From 1808, the overcoat was replaced by a full dress jacket which was more than a year old. The cavalryman also wore over-trousers which fastened on the sides with 16 or 18 buttons.

Young Guard squadron in campaign dress around 1813-1814. The rolled-up coat was worn over the shoulder.

Cavalryman during the Belgian Campaign, in 1815. A Minerva type helmet (helmet like that of the great goddess Minerva), one of the traditional hallmarks of the Dragoons of the Guard, was partly replaced by a model which resembled more that of the *Ancien Régime* Dragoons. As they had become the *'Dragons de France'* in 1814, the Dragoons of the Guard theoretically wore a white aglet, one of the signs of the monarchy which replaced those of the Empire. When Napoleon returned from Elba, they were very rapidly replaced by the Imperial arms, although not everybody had the time to do this.

CLOTHING

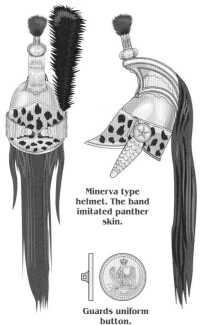

Minerva type helmet. The band imitated panther skin.

Guards uniform button.

Town dress bicorne. It was taller than that of the Grenadiers à cheval.

Forage cap for soldiers and NCOs. Theoretically the NCOs wore the soldiers' forage cap, but it is not impossible for them to have had them made with gold striping at their own expense. The soldiers' forage cap was decorated with white piping from 1812.

Rank markings.
1. Cavalryman with 10-20 years' service.
2. *Brigadier* with more than 20-25 years' service
3. *Brigadier-Fourrier* (with NCO rank)
4. *Maréchal-des-Logis.*
5. *Maréchal-des-Logis-Chef.*

Jacket.

Soldier's contra-epaulette.

NCO's contra-epaulette.

Deerskin breeches.

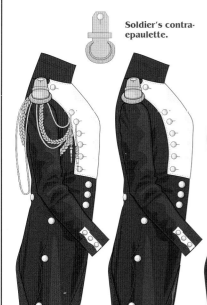

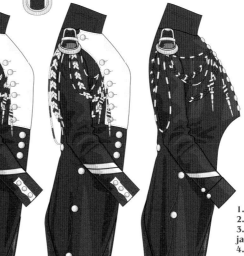

1. Full dress jacket.
2. Young Guard jacket.
3. *Maréchal-des-Logis'* full dress jacket.
4. *Maréchal-des-Logis-Chef's* full dress jacket.
5. *Maréchal-des-Logis'* overcoat.

Note that the scarlet wool slightly mixed with gold became half gold and half scarlet for NCOs at the end of the Empire.

31

ARMAMENT and EQUIPMENT

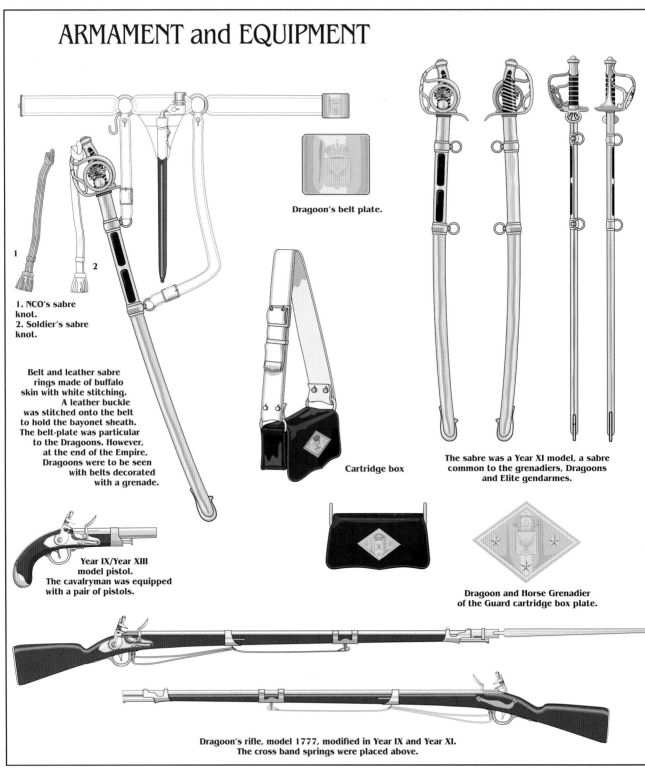

1. NCO's sabre knot.
2. Soldier's sabre knot.

Belt and leather sabre rings made of buffalo skin with white stitching. A leather buckle was stitched onto the belt to hold the bayonet sheath. The belt-plate was particular to the Dragoons. However, at the end of the Empire, Dragoons were to be seen with belts decorated with a grenade.

Dragoon's belt plate.

Cartridge box

The sabre was a Year XI model, a sabre common to the grenadiers, Dragoons and Elite gendarmes.

Year IX/Year XIII model pistol. The cavalryman was equipped with a pair of pistols.

Dragoon and Horse Grenadier of the Guard cartridge box plate.

Dragoon's rifle, model 1777, modified in Year IX and Year XI. The cross band springs were placed above.

SADDLES

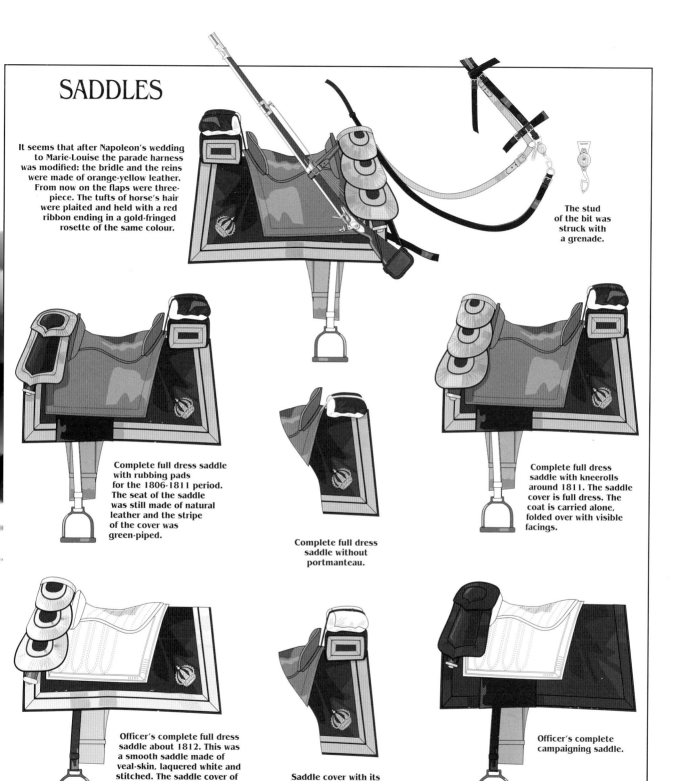

It seems that after Napoleon's wedding to Marie-Louise the parade harness was modified: the bridle and the reins were made of orange-yellow leather. From now on the flaps were three-piece. The tufts of horse's hair were plaited and held with a red ribbon ending in a gold-fringed rosette of the same colour.

The stud of the bit was struck with a grenade.

Complete full dress saddle with rubbing pads for the 1806-1811 period. The seat of the saddle was still made of natural leather and the stripe of the cover was green-piped.

Complete full dress saddle without portmanteau.

Complete full dress saddle with kneerolls around 1811. The saddle cover is full dress. The coat is carried alone, folded over with visible facings.

Officer's complete full dress saddle about 1812. This was a smooth saddle made of veal-skin, laquered white and stitched. The saddle cover of the senior officers would have been edged with three stripes, as were the holster flaps

Saddle cover with its portmanteau, and the coat is folded for marching.

Officer's complete campaigning saddle.

The NCOs

Maréchal-des-Logis wearing an overcoat. He is wearing the same coat with a round-cloak of the first model as the soldiers but his is green.

Maréchal-des-Logis-Fourrier The simple quartermaster was considered as an NCO.

Maréchal-des-Logis wearing full service dress, about 1810.

Maréchal-des-Logis wearing summer town dress.

Maréchal-des-Logis wearing a frock coat, morning dress. The NCOs theoretically wore the same hooded coat as the troops did. Green-coloured coats may have been issued.

Maréchal-des-Logis wearing a frock coat. This item was at the NCOs' expense and was particularly worn by the *Maréchal-des-Logis-chefs*.

TRUMPETERS

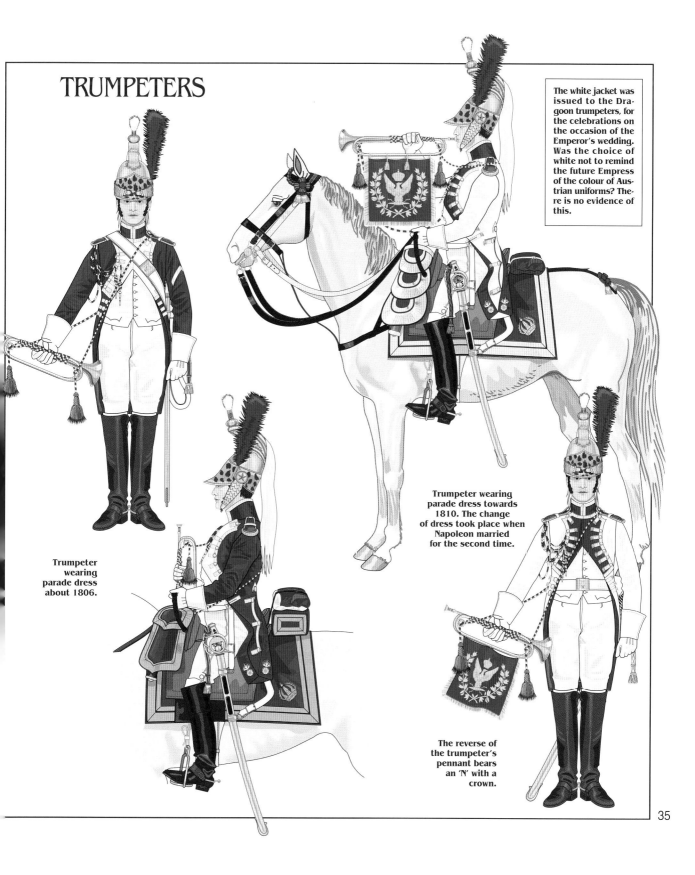

The white jacket was issued to the Dragoon trumpeters, for the celebrations on the occasion of the Emperor's wedding. Was the choice of white not to remind the future Empress of the colour of Austrian uniforms? There is no evidence of this.

Trumpeter wearing parade dress about 1806.

Trumpeter wearing parade dress towards 1810. The change of dress took place when Napoleon married for the second time.

The reverse of the trumpeter's pennant bears an 'N' with a crown.

35

TRUMPETERS

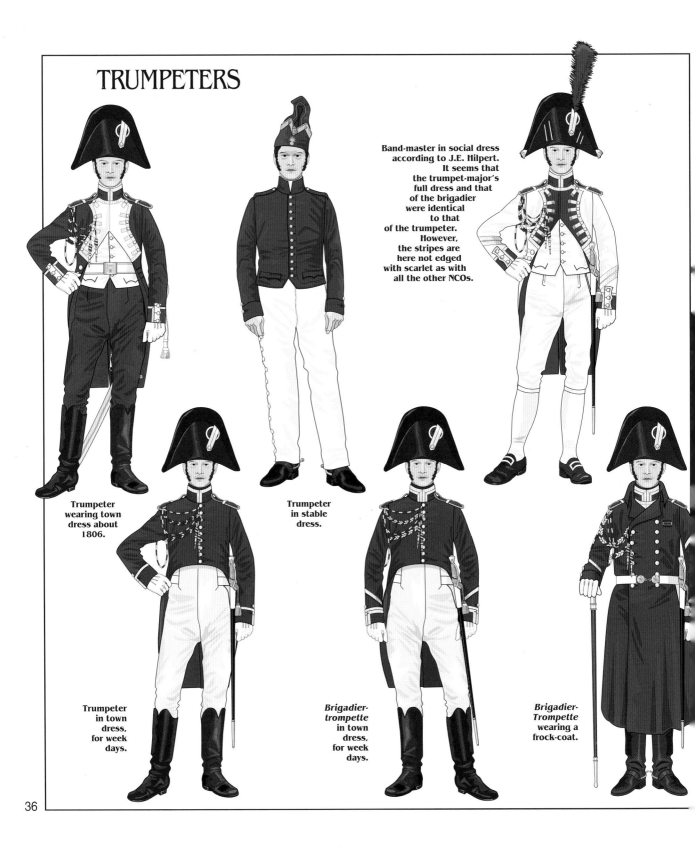

Band-master in social dress according to J.E. Hilpert. It seems that the trumpet-major's full dress and that of the brigadier were identical to that of the trumpeter. However, the stripes are here not edged with scarlet as with all the other NCOs.

Trumpeter wearing town dress about 1806.

Trumpeter in stable dress.

Trumpeter in town dress, for week days.

Brigadier-trompette in town dress, for week days.

Brigadier-Trompette wearing a frock-coat.

36

TRUMPETERS

TTrumpeter wearing an overcoat about 1806. As with the cavalryman, this was the most commonly used campaign dress. The full dress jackets were left at the depots.

Trumpeter in an overcoat towards 1812. It was probably in 1810 that the overcoat got its scarlet coloured collar, which it kept until the end of the Empire.

Trumpeter wearing a coat with a round-cloak, first model.

Trumpeter wearing a coat with a round-cloak, second model, about 1812.

Trumpeter wearing camp dress about 1812.

Strangely, in 1806, in the Dragoons of the Guard, the trumpeter's aglets and contra epaulettes were made of blue silk mixed with silver thread. The choice of this colour may have been inspired by the colour of the brass buttons of the Dragoons of the Line.
In 1808, the silver thread was replaced by one-third gold and two-thirds blue thread.

TRUMPETERS

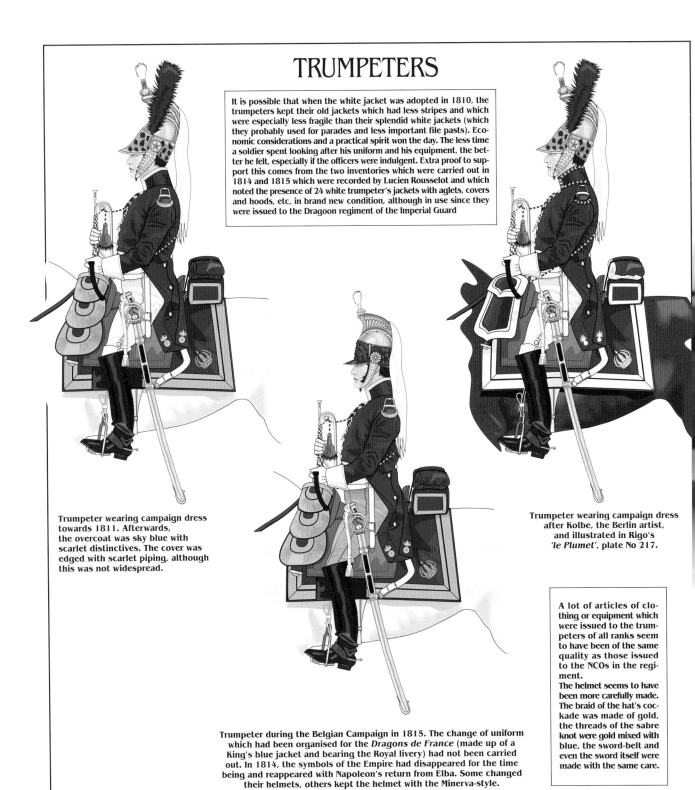

It is possible that when the white jacket was adopted in 1810, the trumpeters kept their old jackets which had less stripes and which were especially less fragile than their splendid white jackets (which they probably used for parades and less important file pasts). Economic considerations and a practical spirit won the day. The less time a soldier spent looking after his uniform and his equipment, the better he felt, especially if the officers were indulgent. Extra proof to support this comes from the two inventories which were carried out in 1814 and 1815 which were recorded by Lucien Rousselot and which noted the presence of 24 white trumpeter's jackets with aglets, covers and hoods, etc, in brand new condition, although in use since they were issued to the Dragoon regiment of the Imperial Guard

Trumpeter wearing campaign dress towards 1811. Afterwards, the overcoat was sky blue with scarlet distinctives. The cover was edged with scarlet piping, although this was not widespread.

Trumpeter wearing campaign dress after Kolbe, the Berlin artist, and illustrated in Rigo's 'le Plumet', plate No 217.

Trumpeter during the Belgian Campaign in 1815. The change of uniform which had been organised for the *Dragons de France* (made up of a King's blue jacket and bearing the Royal livery) had not been carried out. In 1814, the symbols of the Empire had disappeared for the time being and reappeared with Napoleon's return from Elba. Some changed their helmets, others kept the helmet with the Minerva-style.

A lot of articles of clothing or equipment which were issued to the trumpeters of all ranks seem to have been of the same quality as those issued to the NCOs in the regiment.
The helmet seems to have been more carefully made. The braid of the hat's cockade was made of gold, the threads of the sabre knot were gold mixed with blue, the sword-belt and even the sword itself were made with the same care.

CLOTHING and EQUIPMENT

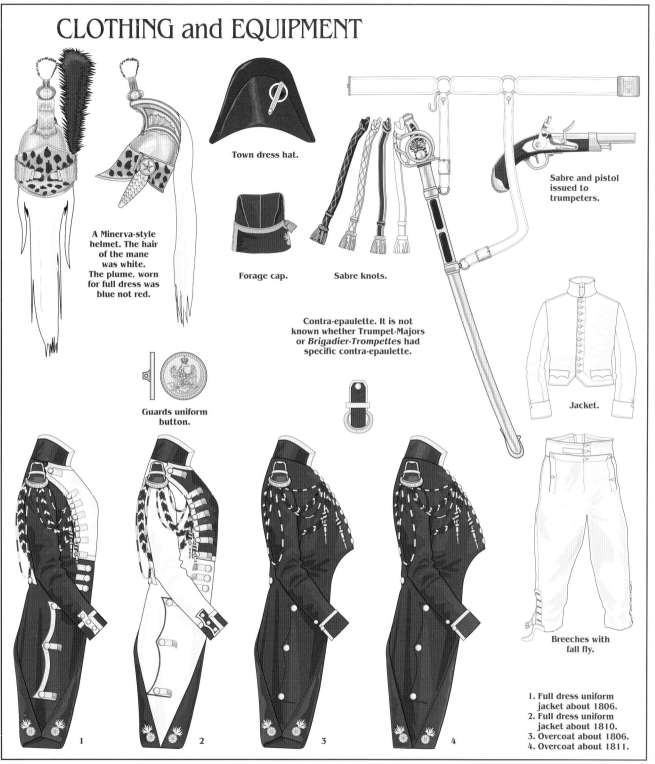

A Minerva-style
helmet. The hair
of the mane
was white.
The plume, worn
for full dress was
blue not red.

Town dress hat.

Forage cap.

Sabre knots.

Sabre and pistol
issued to
trumpeters.

Contra-epaulette. It is not
known whether Trumpet-Majors
or *Brigadier-Trompettes* had
specific contra-epaulette.

Guards uniform
button.

Jacket.

Breeches with
fall fly.

1. Full dress uniform
   jacket about 1806.
2. Full dress uniform
   jacket about 1810.
3. Overcoat about 1806.
4. Overcoat about 1811.

1   2   3   4

The KETTLEDRUMMER

This coloured kettledrummer
in full dress about 1808.
Note the way the horse is directed,
by fixing the reins to the stirrups.
Lucien Rousselot and Rigo presented
him like this even though the archives
mention three Frenchmen in the Dragoons employed
as kettledrummers without mentioning
the colour of their skin.
The kettledrummer used drums rather than timpani.
This apparent oddity was revealed by the shape
and the size of the drums and their aprons.
The drummers preserved the tradition of the Ancien Régime.
The kettledrummer here is dressed in the Turkish style,
according to a fashion already established at the time.
The horse is being led on foot because the reins
were fixed to the stirrups.

Where the kettledrummer is concerned, the regimental archives of the Dragoons of the Imperial Guard mention that three Frenchmen in turn had the position, without any mention being made of the colour of their skin. It can be reasonably assumed, given the administrative habits of the period, that if one or all of the drummers had been coloured, the documents would have mentioned this fact. The picture then that is in the Alsatian Collection is therefore probably mistaken. It was however taken up by Eugène Lelièpvre, Lucien Rousselot and Rigo, but with the usual reservations.

Kettledrummer, on foot in full dress.
The oriental-style sabres, Turkish dress, the turbans,
and Egyptian fashion lasted a long time in the Guard,
as it did in the *Grande Armée*.

40

The OFFICERS

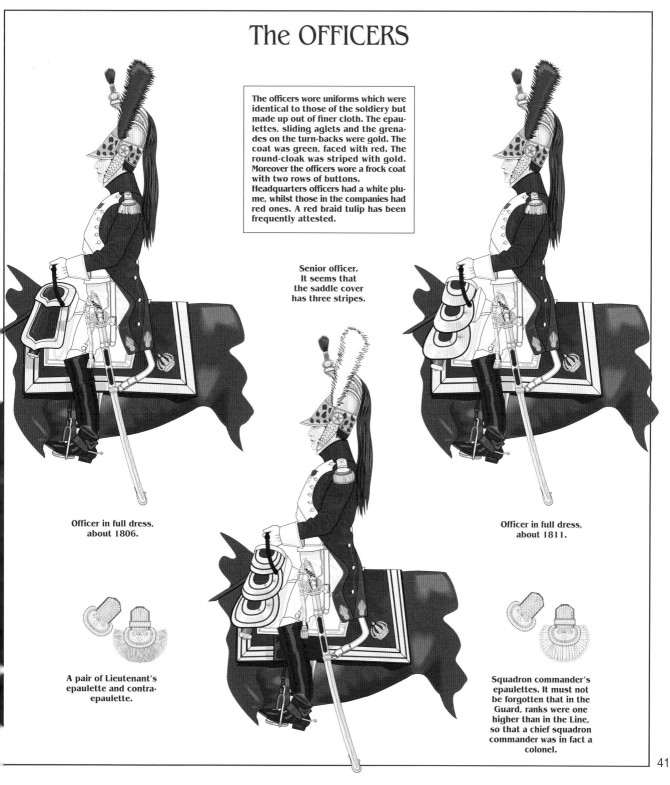

The officers wore uniforms which were identical to those of the soldiery but made up out of finer cloth. The epaulettes, sliding aglets and the grenades on the turn-backs were gold. The coat was green, faced with red. The round-cloak was striped with gold. Moreover the officers wore a frock coat with two rows of buttons.
Headquarters officers had a white plume, whilst those in the companies had red ones. A red braid tulip has been frequently attested.

Senior officer.
It seems that
the saddle cover
has three stripes.

Officer in full dress,
about 1806.

Officer in full dress,
about 1811.

A pair of Lieutenant's
epaulette and contra-
epaulette.

Squadron commander's
epaulettes. It must not
be forgotten that in the
Guard, ranks were one
higher than in the Line,
so that a chief squadron
commander was in fact a
colonel.

TOWN and QUARTERS DRESS

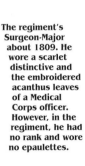

Officer in
summer
town
dress.

Officer in summer
social dress.

Officer in morning
dress, wearing
a coat.

Officer in morning
dress, wearing
an overcoat.

The regiment's
Surgeon-Major
about 1809. He
wore a scarlet
distinctive and
the embroidered
acanthus leaves
of a Medical
Corps officer.
However, in the
regiment, he had
no rank and wore
no epaulettes.

The strength of the regiment
in 1811.

There was one headquarters and 5
two-company squadrons of
Dragoons, 80 officers and 1 210
men.

The headquarters was made up of:
1 Colonel (in fact a Major-General).
2 Majors.
1 Instruction Squadron Commander.
1 Quartermaster-treasurer.
1 Instructor Captain.
2 Adjudant-Majors.
5 Under-Adjudant -Majors.
4 Guidon-bearers.
3 Adjudant-Lieutenants
    (*Administration*)
2 Surgeon - Majors
3 Assistant Surgeon-Majors.
1 *Maréchal-des-Logis*
    Under -Instructor.

1 *Maréchal-des-Logis-Chef*
Quartermaster.
2 Vets.
4 Assistant Vets.
1 Trumpet-Major.
1 *Brigadier-Timbalist.*
2 *Brigadier-Trompettes.*
6 Master-craftsmen.
2 Blacksmiths.

At that date, each company
was made up of

1 Captain
2 First-Lieutenants.
2 Second-Lieutenants
1 *Maréchaux-des-Logis-Chef.*
6 *Maréchaux-des-Logis.*
1 Quartermaster.
10 *Brigadiers.*
2 Blacksmiths.
3 Trumpeters.
96 Dragoons.

OFFICER'S CAMPAIGN DRESS

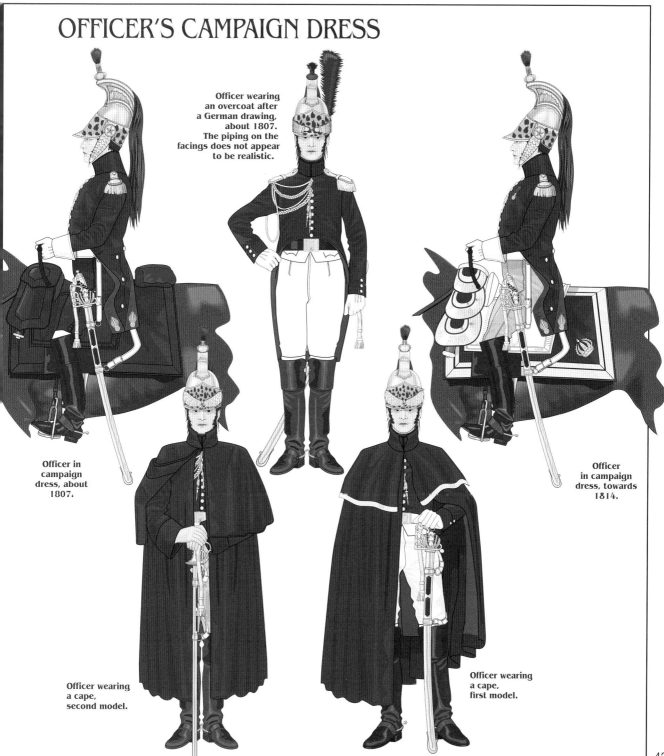

Officer wearing
an overcoat after
a German drawing,
about 1807.
The piping on the
facings does not appear
to be realistic.

Officer in
campaign
dress, about
1807.

Officer
in campaign
dress, towards
1814.

Officer wearing
a cape,
second model.

Officer wearing
a cape,
first model.

The *GUIDONS* and the EAGLES

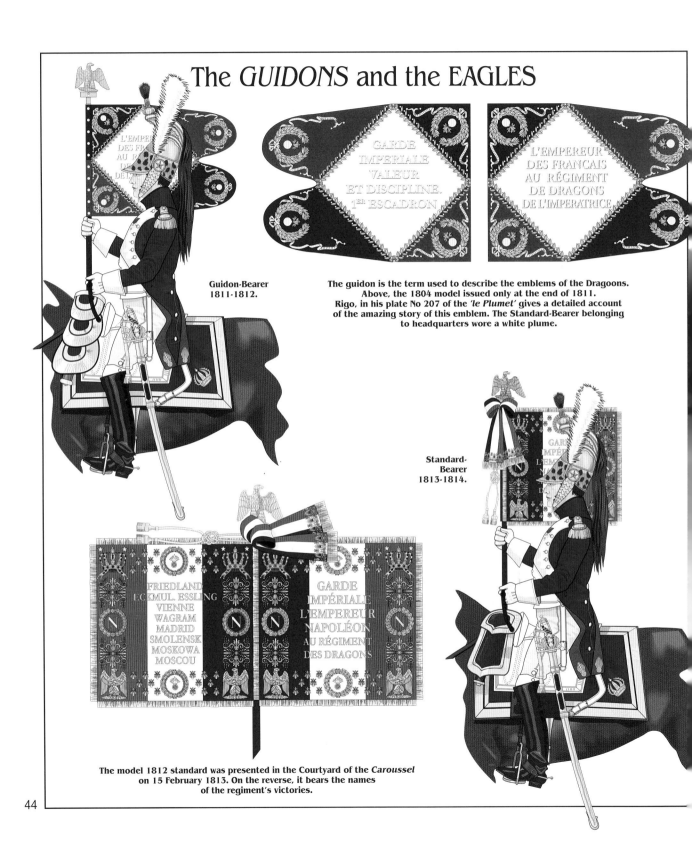

**Guidon-Bearer
1811-1812.**

GARDE
IMPÉRIALE
VALEUR
ET DISCIPLINE.
1ᴱᴿ ESCADRON

L'EMPEREUR
DES FRANCAIS
AU RÉGIMENT
DE DRAGONS
DE L'IMPERATRICE

The guidon is the term used to describe the emblems of the Dragoons.
Above, the 1804 model issued only at the end of 1811.
Rigo, in his plate No 207 of the *'le Plumet'* gives a detailed account
of the amazing story of this emblem. The Standard-Bearer belonging
to headquarters wore a white plume.

**Standard-
Bearer
1813-1814.**

FRIEDLAND
ECKMUL. ESSLING
VIENNE
WAGRAM
MADRID
SMOLENSK
MOSKOWA
MOSCOU

GARDE
IMPÉRIALE
L'EMPEREUR
NAPOLÉON
AU RÉGIMENT
DES DRAGONS

**The model 1812 standard was presented in the Courtyard of the *Caroussel*
on 15 February 1813. On the reverse, it bears the names
of the regiment's victories.**

44

The OFFICERS COMMANDING

In February 1813, Major-General Antoine d'Ornano was appointed
Colonel of the Regiment of Dragoons of the Guard.
It was because of this that he wore a general's distinctions
on his Dragoon uniform. The equipment is that of a general
with a crimson saddle cover. However, Rigo, on Plate No 58
gave him with the saddle of a senior officer.
Count Ornano was an *Officier* of the *Légion
d'Honneur* and after 1813 wore the plate
of the *Grande Croix de l'Ordre de la Réunion*
whose sky-blue ribbon was worn saltire-wise.
The General was a count of the Empire.

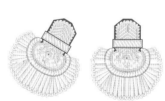

Epaulettes
of the *Major*
(Brigadier in the Line)
baron de Pinteville.

Count Ornano's Jacket.
There were a double
row of oak leaves
on the collar,
and braid twists
on the epaulettes
bearing the three silver
stars. His red and gold
cummerbund scarf and
a jacket whose turn
backs and waist were
decorated
with oak leaves.

This uniform has been taken
from a portrait of Baron
de Pinteville which is kept
in Toul Museum.
He was Colonel
of the 30th Regiment
of Dragoons and appointed
Major in the Regiment
of the Dragoons of the Guard
on 3 February 1813.
He was promoted to Honorary
Maréchal de Camp
(the equivalent of a Brigadier),
on 24 January 1815 by Louis
XVIII, confirmed and retired with
that rank on 3 June 1815.
This is perhaps the reason for him
being presented on this painting
wearing a second dress uniform,
decorated with a brigadier's oak
leaves as well as epaulettes with
two stars. He was an Officier
of the *Légion d'Honneur*
and a *Baron* of the Empire.

Epaulettes of the Colonel-
Commandant of the Regiment of the
Dragoons of the Guard in 1813.

The REGIMENT'S BATTLES

— **1807**, the régiment fought at
the battles of Eylau and Friedland
— **1808,** the regiment is in
Spain.
— **In 1809**, Dragoons were a
part of the *Armée d'Allemagne*,
They were at Wagram but they
didn't fought.
— **In 1810**, two squadrons
fought in Spain.
—**In 1812**, with the Great Army,
during the Russain Campaign
— **In1813**, they fought at the
battles of Bautzen, Wachau and
Leipzig.
— **In 1814**, they fought at Brien-
ne, Champaubert, Montmirail,
Château-Thierry, Vauchamps, Mon-
tereau, Reims, Craonne, Arcis-sur-
Aube, Saint-Dizier and Paris.
— **In 1815**, they are at Ligny
and Waterloo.

The CHASSEURS à CHEVAL

Because of their Egyptian and Italian background, the *Chasseurs à Cheval* of the Imperial Guard, were the units which knew their famous leader best. They had been by his side from the beginning and felt responsible for his person.

Moreover, because their duty created its own ethos, they inherited all the traditions of the Light Cavalry: bravery, boastfulness, resourcefulness, gaiety and total devotion. They became the model for the light cavalry, even within this elite unit.

It was for all those reasons, and for many others, that Napoleon liked them, spoilt them and preferred them to all the others.

The Chasseurs knew this, as did all the *Grande Armée*, and took advantage of it. From their beginning up to the times of Imperial glory, was not their commander Eugène de Beauharnais, the Emperor's own bubbling and impetuous beloved son-in-law.

The Chasseurs à Cheval.

The *Compagnie des Chasseurs à Cheval de la Garde des Consuls* (the Company of the Chasseurs à Cheval of the Consular Guard), set up on *13 Nivose An VIII* (13 January 1800) was at the origins of the *Chasseurs à Cheval* of the Guard.

The backbone of the company was made up of old guides of the general who had been in command in Egypt.

The company became a squadron with two companies by Consular Decree of 8 September 1800. A year later, on 6 August 1801, the corps went up to two two-company squadrons. The two squadrons finally became a regiment on 14 November of the same year.

On 1 October 1802, the regiment grew from two squadrons to four. When the Consular Guard became the Imperial Guard on 21 January 1804, the Mameluks (see our forthcoming volume three) were attached to the *Chasseurs à Cheval*. The regiment took up its final name: *Chasseurs à Cheval de la Garde Impériale* (*Chasseurs à Cheval* of the Imperial Guard) on 18 May 1804, without changing its composition.

On 17 September 1805, a four-company squadron

The REGIMENT'S STRENGTH

In 1804, the regiment had a headquarters and four squadrons with two companies. In the headquarters there were:

A squadron commander, an *adjudant-major*, four standard-bearers, a Trumpet-Major, a kettledrummer, a brigadier-trompette and four master-craftsmen.

Each company theoretically included a captain commanding the company, a first-lieutenant, a second-lieutenant and a *'sous-lieutenant'* (another second lieutenant); a *maréchal-des-logis chef*, four *maréchaux-des-logis*, one *brigadier-fourrier*, eight *brigadiers*, one blacksmith, two trumpeters and eighty-four *chasseurs à cheval*.

---

of Velites was added to the strength (the decree made provision for 400 men) of the existing squadrons. On 15 April 1806, a second squadron of Velites joined the first.

In December 1809, the Velites were reorganised in one single squadron with two companies.

The Russian Campaign obliged the regiment to be increased to five squadrons of Old Guard. On this occasion the Velites disappeared and joined once and for all their elders. In 1813, after the disastrous retreat from Russia, the Guard was reorganised and the regiment of *Chasseurs à Cheval* of the Guard was given eight squadrons among which three from the Young Guard. The chasseurs lost almost 5000 men in the Russian Campaign.

During the first Restoration, the Chasseurs became the *Corps Royal des Chasseurs à Cheval de France*. At that time, it had four two-company squadrons. The Hundred Days, with the return of the Emperor (which did not modify the make-up of the regiment) saw the regiment become the Regiment of *Chasseurs à Cheval* of the Imperial Guard once again. It was wearing a rather less glamorous uniform than formerly that they entered Belgium.

The first light cavalrymen of the Imperial Guard were finally dismissed in October and November 1815 at Périgueux.

The Velites

As with the other units of the Cavalry in the Imperial Guard, the Velites of the *Chasseurs à Cheval* were recruited among the sons of the bourgeoisie who could prove they had an annual income of three hundred francs, buy their own uniform and be of the required height.

When the regiment left on campaign, the Velites were spread out among the battle companies. For the Velites in the Chasseurs, there was the possibility, at the end of three years' service of joining a regiment of the Old Guard or being appointed NCO in a regiment of the Line.

Some, among the best, could even be promoted to officer rank directly in a cavalry regiment of the Line.

Music in the Chasseurs à Cheval.

The band was mainly made up of trumpeters but did have a kettledrummer. The company of the *Chasseurs à Cheval* of the Consular Guard originally had only two trumpeters.

In September 1800, with its two-company squadron, the corps numbered four trumpeters. With its two two-company squadrons, the number of trumpeters went up to eight.

In 1802, the organisation of the regiment made for three trumpeters per company (so twelve in all for the corps). They were under the orders of a trumpet-major and two *brigadiers trompettes*.

At the end of 1802, when there were four squadrons, the trumpeters increased to twenty-four, to which must be added the three NCOs. In 1811, on the creation of the 5th squadron, there were 30 trumpeters (ten companies of Old Guard with three trumpeters spread out among five squadrons), to which must added the twenty-four trumpeters of the four squadrons of the Young Guard in 1813.

The first kettledrummer of the regiment was a fourteen-year-old youth who died in 1,808in Madrid. During parades and march pasts he had the great honour of opening up the march for the regiment. The kettledrummer who had the rank of *Brigadier-Trompette* was part of headquarters.

His splendid Turkish-style uniform can be seen on pages 69-70 of this volume.

Travelling light in the Light Cavalry.

The coat was placed over the front of the saddle covering the holsters and itself was covered by the round-cloak. Cavalrymen were advised to wear it saltire-wise during charges to protect the body. The haversack was fixed onto the left holster. Behind the cantle, on the saddle-cloth the *chasseur à cheval* placed the forage bag folded under the portmanteau.

Normally on campaign this contained two shirts, two ties, two handkerchiefs, breeches or trousers, a waistcoat, a forage cap, stable jacket, a second pair of boots and a toilet bag.

Some famous names...

In 1806, Prince Eugène de Beauharnais, Major-General, commanded the *Chasseurs à Cheval*.

Colonel Dahlmann was second-in-command, Colonel Guyot was the regimental Major.

The squadron commanders were the younger Clerc, Bohn, Thiry, Francq, Daumesnil and Cavrois.

In 1813, Lefebvre-Desnouettes (who had suggested a red plume which was very quickly abandoned in favour of the red green-tipped plume) was a Major-General and commanded the regiment.

Brigadier Baron Guyot was the second in command and Colonel Baron Lion was the regimental Major.

The squadron commanders were respectively Chevalier Joanes, Rabusson, Chevalier Bayeux, Labiffe, Lafitte, Vanot, Debelle, Trobriant, Guiotand Cavre.

The REGIMENT'S BATTLES

From 1805 to 1807, the regiment accompanied the Emperor and took part in the battles of Austerlitz, Lopaczyn, Eylau and Guttstadt. During the battle of Jena-Auerstadt, the regiment was not with the Emperor; it was the 7th Hussars which acted as Napoleon's bodyguard.

In 1808, they fought at the Battle of Benevente.

In 1809, the Chasseurs were with the army in Germany and even if they did not participate in the Battle of Wagram, they were there.

In 1811-12, a detachment of the Chasseurs was in Spain at Elione.

In 1812, with the Grande Armée they fought at Malojaroslawetz.

In 1813, still with the Grande Armée they fought at the battles of Reichenbach, Dresden, Leipzig, Weimar and Hanau.

In 1814, they fought at Château-Thierry, Craonne and Valcourt.

In 1815, they fought at Coutrai and Waterloo.

FULL DRESS

Chasseur à Cheval of the Guard
in full dress.
This was Hussar-style dress made
up principally of a black bearskin
colback, a dolman,
a woollen cummerbund,
deerskin breeches,
a scarlet cloth pelisse
with a black sheepskin edge,
a light cavalry sabre
(especially for the Guard),
a richly decorated sabretache
and a pair
of Suvarov-style boots.

In full dress,
the pelisse was
worn over
the left shoulder
and held there with
a cord. Harnessing
was 'Hungarian-style'
and typical of all light
cavalry units.
The Chasseurs wore
their hair long in
a ponytail,
a moustache
and wore gold
ear-rings.

Cavalryman
in full dress about 1808.
Front and back.
The *Chasseur à cheval*
only had one
pair of short gloves.
However
at the beginning
of the period,
the cavalrymen also
wore gauntlets
on parade.

Cavarlyman in full
mounted service dress,
about 1808.

It was probably around 1802, that the dolman and the pelisse were given
five rows of buttons which remained until the end of the Empire. Indeed
at this date, the grand uniform of the *Chasseurs à Cheval* of the Guard
was fixed more or less definitely. The major changes which were made
to the uniform only concerned the emblems to be seen on the different
items of the uniform or equipment, e.g. turnbacks, sabretaches, shabracks, cartridge boxes, etc.
Winter full dress was made up of the pelisse. In summer, the Chasseur à
Cheval wore a dolman and wore a loose pelisse over the left shoulder.
From 1802, in both winter and summer deerskin breeches replaced the
scarlet Hungarian-style breeches from the beginning of the period of the
Consuls. The full dress colback was always worn with the plume, and the
sabretache was not protected by its sheath.

FULL DRESS

Unlike their brothers-in-arms the Dragoons and the Grenadiers à cheval, the *Chasseurs à Cheval* did not have many pairs of boots. The Hungarian-style boots were folded at the ankle and the top of the leg had a square braid and aurora-yellow tassel hanging from the point of the heart-shaped serration. The spurs were screwed into the heel; they were made of bronzed iron later replaced by brass with an iron rowel around 1808, as the price of raw materials had soared because of the shortage of supplies due to the Blockade.

Cavalryman in full dress, around 1805. Ever since the Consular Guard, headpieces were less voluminous and did not have a visor. The cockade on the colback did not have an eagle in its centre at the beginning of the Empire. The deerskin breeches replaced the Hungarian-style scarlet breeches. The corners of the shabrack were decorated with a little horn. There were tufts originally but they were removed. The arms of the Empire replaced those of the Consular period in the centre of the sabretache.

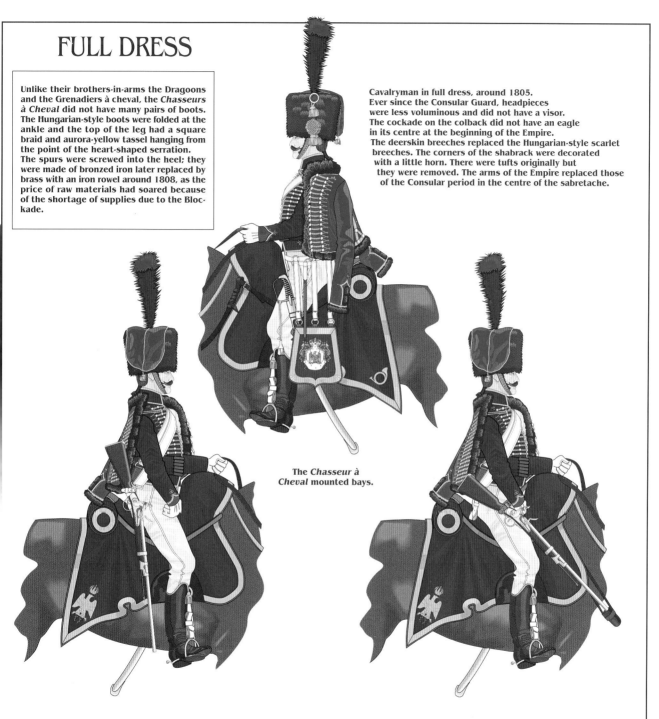

The *Chasseur à Cheval* mounted bays.

Cavalryman seen from the offside.
(The right hand side, away from the horse block).
These two chasseurs are showing the two regulation ways of wearing the carbine (in fact a 1786 musket): either hanging from the musket strap and held by its strap (*left*); or with the barrel stuck into the saddle holster and held by a strap (*right*).

TOWN DRESS

Town dress was differentiated by the seasons: from May to September it was called 'Summer', from October to April it as called 'Winter'.
Moreover, there was different dress for Sundays and weekdays and this dress was always worn with the hat and plume, whatever the basic uniform (coat, pelisse or dolman).

Summer town dress. The cavalryman is wearing the jacket 'à la Chasseur'. In this get-up, the sabretache was never worn with the sabre.

Summer town dress for Sundays.
The dolman was worn on a braided waistcoat fastened only by the top buttons to let the latter's richly decorated facings show.

Summer town dress.
The tail coat was worn with a waistcoat and nankeen or white cotton breeches without any particular ornament. The coat and the waistcoat had the same cut as the plain jacket and the green Hungarian breeches of the basic uniform.

Winter town dress, pelisse worn over the waistcoat.
The sabre was worn without the sabretache.

— Regulation Sunday town dress in winter was made up of the pelisse, the braided waistcoat, the green Hungarian breeches and the sabre worn without the sabretache.
— Town dress for weekdays in winter from October to April consisted of the coat instead of the pelisse. The rest did not change.
— Sunday town dress in April was made up of the dolman, the green Hungarian breeches and the sabretache. Weekday dress was exactly the same as for winter.
— From May to September, on Sundays, the cavalrymen wore the green dolman, the waistcoat and the green nankeen, the breeches, the little sabre and the sabretache. During the week, the chasseur donned the waistcoat and the nankeen breeches. The sabretache was not worn.
— The 'à la Souvarov' boots and the bicorne with a plume were worn in all cases.

50

QUARTERS DRESS

Quarters dress can be considered the same as stable dress, or dress worn within the barracks. This varied with what the cavalryman had at his disposal and what the orders of the day were.

Dress consisting of waistcoat and gaiters, around 1805.

Dress with stable waistcoat and white twill trousers, called stable trousers, around 1805.

Dress with stable waistcoat and Riding breeches for walking the horse, around 1813.

Quarters dress towards 1808, with a pelisse and forage cap.

The *Chasseurs à Cheval*'s coat was probably originally this very loose coat made of green cloth, with a collar and a small cape which was issued to a greater or lesser degree in this form throughout the cavalry. The first type of coat had no sleeves. The chasseurs were issued with a cape coat with sleeves and a round-cloak towards 1812.
It seems that it was not worn very often by the cavalrymen.
In 1804, the *Chasseurs à Cheval* of the Consular Guard were issued with big round-cloaks, replacing the little ones on the existing coats. This removable cape was used in case of bad weather according to the circumstances - picket duty with the First Consul - where coats were not allowed.
This round-cloak had a short life apparently and by 1807, the coat probably no longer had a removable cape.
The NCOs (see below) seemed to have been issued with a specific cape-coat.

Brigadier in quarters dress, around 1808. He is wearing the coat '*à la Chasseur*' and the Riding breeches with red stripes down the sides.

QUARTERS DRESS

Unlike the preceding dress, these soldiers have been inspired by a period drawing realised by Lieutenant J.-M. Chevalier, who joined the *Chasseurs à Cheval* in 1808 as *Maréchal-des-Logis-Chef* and remained there until 1815. These colour drawings were published in the first number of *'Tradition Magazine'*. They show a barrack room and a guardroom with a number of Chasseurs wearing a jacket which we have tried to reproduce below. The stripes on the coat were drawn like those of the pelisse, which seems a little unlikely.

Stable or Quarters dress.
The jacket bears a row of nine buttons or even twelve. The pointed facings do not have buttons, the pockets were piped like the front. A pair of cloth shoulder straps have been put onto this jacket. The forage cap is identical to the models given by other sources.

The forage cap unlike the hat, did not change shape or size during the regiment's fifteen-year existence. It was made of cloth of the colour attributed to the *Chasseurs* of the Guard.
The turban was striped with aurora yellow, sometimes edged with scarlet. Decorated with a little yellow woollen horn on the front, it was also decorated with a flame of the same colour as the background cloth. The seams, numbering four were covered by yellow braid.
The stable waistcoat was made of cloth and was crossed over the breast with two rows of ten yellow buttons.
The canvas stable trousers opened on each side over the whole length and was closed on each leg by a row of 18 bone buttons.

Brigadier wearing a jacket and Riding breeches with red stripes on the sides.
The brigadier's stripes follow the shape of the facings. However they could also be straight, chevron-shaped.

Cavalryman in quarters dress.

CAMPAIGN DRESS with the COAT

Cavalryman wearing the coat *'à la Chasseur'* towards 1805. He is wearing Riding breeches with the red side stripe and with a plain waistcoat.

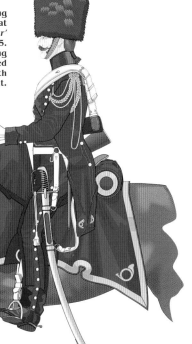

Cavalryman wearing a chasseur coat around 1807, during the Polish Campaign.

The coat was the second uniform of the chasseurs. It was used in all circumstances in order to preserve the full dress 'à la Hussarde' uniform.
Nevertheless, it was worn during the first campaigns of the Empire before being replaced by the second uniform dolman and pelisse from the beginning of the Spanish Campaign onwards.
The Chasseur-style coat was still worn as quarters dress and town dress.

Brigadier in campaign dress with the coat and the cloth shabrack.

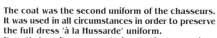

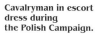

Cavalryman in escort dress during the Polish Campaign.

CAMPAIGN DRESS, 1805-1808

Chasseurs' dress on the eve of Austerlitz, according to Bacler d'Albe.
The cavalryman is wearing the round-cloak of his coat over his pelisse.
The equipment is made up of a saddle and sheepskin shabrack, already parts of the campaign dress during the Consular period.

Dress worn by the *Chasseurs à Cheval* during the great charge of the Cavalry of the Guard at Austerlitz, on 2 December 1805. The coat was worn over the shoulder as individual protection during cavalry charges.

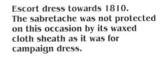

Escort dress towards 1810. The sabretache was not protected on this occasion by its waxed cloth sheath as it was for campaign dress.

Escort and picket dress were defined thus: pelisse chaussée or dolman, according to the orders or the time of year, deerskin breeches, sabretache in its waxed cloth sheath and colback.
But from six o'clock at night, the cavalrymen on picket duty could wear riding breeches and equip their mounts with the green cloth with the black leather surcingle (N.B. the brown leather surcingle was strictly for parade dress only).
On foot picket duty, the chasseur kept this dress but took the sabretache from its sheath. During bad weather, he was allowed to protect his colback with its sheath or scabbard made of waxed taffetas used for just this.
In this case, of course, the plume could not be worn and was also put away in its waxed sheath.
These campaign dispositions were applicable to all periods except perhaps for the German and Polish Campaigns (1806-07), during which the *Chasseurs* wore cloth coats, waistcoats and trousers.

CAMPAIGN DRESS, 1808-1812

The colback which is presented here is that which was brought out in 1803. Its rigid leather structure was covered with black bearskin. It was very slightly cone-shaped, 25 cms high in the front and 27.5 cms behind; it had a leather inside. Its upper diameter was 25 cms in theory.

It had two leather chin straps covered with a brass curb chain. They were attached by means of a short cord which ended each strap. These latter were probably removable and could be moved backwards and be fixed to a leather button hole placed on the back of the headpiece. The scarlet flame whose contours were covered with aurora yellow cord was fixed on the top of the colback.

A plume carrier fob was fixed on the left side of the headpiece and could take a cockade pompom. The yellow woollen cord ended with two flounders, which themselves ended in two tassels and formed an eye through which the stem of the plume or the pom-pom was threaded.

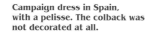

Campaign dress in Spain, with a pelisse. The colback was not decorated at all.

Campaign dress at Wagram in 1809. As protection, the sabretache was slipped into a black waxed canvas sheath without ornament. There was also a sheath made of waxed canvas to protect the colback in case of rain.

The *brigadiers* in the *Chasseurs à Cheval* wore the same clothes as the soldiers.

The seniority stripes were made of aurora yellow-coloured wool. Only the rank stripes worn as chevrons on both sleeves and also made of yellow wool, distinguished the *brigadiers* from the men.

These stripes were worn on the sleeves of the dolman, the pelisse and the coat. Moreover, the brigadiers had an axe sheath instead of the right holster on the saddle.

All the rest of the *brigadier*'s equipment was the same. The NCOs did not have a carbine and so did not wear a musket strap nor a bayonet. The NCO's equipment was otherwise the same as the soldier's.

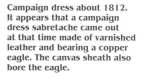

Campaign dress about 1812. It appears that a campaign dress sabretache came out at that time made of varnished leather and bearing a copper eagle. The canvas sheath also bore the eagle.

CAMPAIGN DRESS, 1812-1815

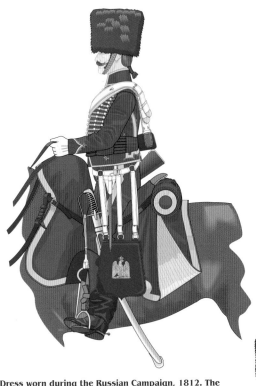

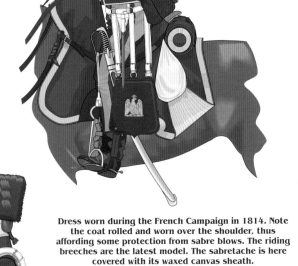

Dress worn during the Russian Campaign, 1812. The cavalryman is wearing trousers with false leather boots which do not seem to have been taken up subsequently. The points of the shabrack have been taken up and fixed below the portmanteau.

Dress worn during the French Campaign in 1814. Note the coat rolled and worn over the shoulder, thus affording some protection from sabre blows. The riding breeches are the latest model. The sabretache is here covered with its waxed canvas sheath.

Dress worn during the Belgium Campaign in 1815. The absence of eagles at the corners of the shabrack is due to the first Restoration when all the symbols of the Empire were removed and replaced by those of the Monarchy.

In 1812 and ever since the Austrian Campaign, the chasseurs wore their dolman when campaigning and no longer wore the deerskin breeches. The Hungarian green cloth breeches or riding breeches replaced them in all circumstances. In 1815 campaign dress was simplified even further, the chasseurs no longer wearing the breeches but the riding breeches. They wore neither plume nor colback cord. The Chasseurs of the Emperor's escort could no longer be distinguished from their brother-in-arms in the regiment except by wearing the colback pennant.

The colback sheath cover was made of waxed canvas and varnished, and also protected the pennant which was itself folded under the scabbard. It was shut by hooking it over the top.

CAMPAIGN DRESS

The coat with long skirts at the beginning of the Empire and its turn-backs were hooked.
Fashion was all-important, even and especially in the Guard; the turn-backs became just mere patches on the skirts; a green triangle was sown on the base cloth and the skirts were shortened.
This triangle disappeared towards 1810 when the turn backs were joined together.
The skirts got narrower and narrower leaving less space for the turn-backs, the front overlapped the point of the rear. The neckline at the front of the coat made a wider angle.

Wearing a coat 'à la Chasseur', the cavalryman's equipment was the same as for full dress.

Cavalryman wearing a coat with a simple waistcoat which at the beginning of the Empire had two rows of buttons. The grey riding breeches had a red strip down the sides.

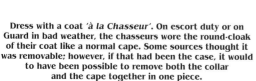

Dress with a coat 'à la Chasseur'. On escort duty or on Guard in bad weather, the chasseurs wore the round-cloak of their coat like a normal cape. Some sources thought it was removable; however, if that had been the case, it would to have been possible to remove both the collar and the cape together in one piece.

Cavalryman wearing a cape-coat in use towards the end of the Empire.

57

CAMPAIGN DRESS

Velite wearing campaign dress, 1805-1810. The Velites of the chasseurs were organised like those of the other regiments of Grenadiers and Dragoons. Their uniform was identical to that of the chasseurs of the Old Guard but made of lesser quality cloth. The strappings were not stitched. The Velite wore a hat instead of a colback and wore his hair short. Armament was the same as the chasseurs' in the older companies. Equipment was that of the old Consular Guard.

Chasseur à Cheval wearing campaign dress and a pelisse, about 1807-1808.

Chasseurs à Cheval in campaign dress and *pelisse chaussée*, after 1812

Chasseurs à Cheval wearing campaign dress, front and back.

The green horse breeches were worn during the campaigns towards the middle of the Empire. The so-called 'Marengo grey' riding breeches, were often worn after the Russian Campaign. This item had a red stripe down the side. Another model without the leather bazan protection and fitted with a system of buttons at the bottom to free the boots has also been attested.

Summer campaign dress. Only the dolman was worn with the green Hungarian breeches. The colback appeared to be fitted with different accessories depending on the circumstances.

CLOTHING

The pennant of the colback was scarlet with patches of aurora yellow, the tassel which ended it was the same colour for the soldiers.

Soldier's forage cap. The NCOs wore the same hat but it had a gold stripe and horn.

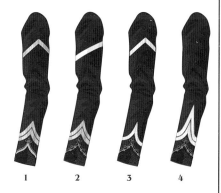

1   2   3   4

Marks of Rank
1. *Brigadier* with 10 to 20 years' service.
2. *Brigadier-Fourrier* who had the rank of NCO
3. *Maréchal-des-Logis* with one seniority stripe
4. *Maréchal-des-Logis-Chef.*
Some sources show the NCOs' stripes edged with scarlet piping.

The bearskin colback took up more space than the one used at the time of the Consular Guard. From 1806, a yellow embroidered eagle was added to the cockade.
The NCO's headpiece had a gold and green raquette with gold and green braid on the pennant. The NCOs also had an eagle embroidered on the cockade.

Cavalryman's pelisse upon which there are a brigadier's rank and yellow woollen seniority stripes.
Below the NCO's pelisse was decorated with green and gold braid.
The fur used was the marmot's.

Cavalryman's dolman with 18 lines of braid.
The stripes are decorated with yellow Russian woollen braid for which the designs vary quite a bit depending on the models.
The NCO's dolman on the right has scarlet and gold braid, like the flat fringes.

The cummerbund was decorated with woollen webs fitted with scarlet loops. The NCOs had the same but with scarlet and gold loops.

Front view of a dolman. The inside of the dolman was lined with cloth, the bottom was however reinforced with a strip of leather. The pointed facings closed with hooks.

Full dress deerskin breeches. This was common to all the men in the corps.

CLOTHING

Shoulder trefoil.

The town dress hat was issued to the Velites. With fashion, the hat got taller.
The loops of the wings were made of yellow wool, green and gold for the officers.
The green plume worn with this headpiece was the same as for full dress,
but mounted on a more supple stiffener.

The turn-backs were decorated with yellow embroidered horns.

The waistscoat was decorated with yellow braid; there
were some models in existence which had a scarlet collar
braided with gold and decorated sometimes with
trimmings. The chasseurs also used a simple waistcoat,
buttoning straight up or with a double row of buttons.

Shoulder trefoil.

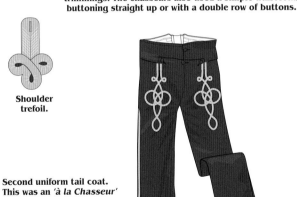

Skirts with straight turn-backs.

Second uniform tail coat.
This was an 'à la Chasseur'
coat with pointed lapels
and facings and
'à la Soubise' pockets.
For the Guard, it was
decorated with an yellow
clover-leaf aiglet.
On the other shoulder,
there is a clover leaf made
of yellow wool braid.
The braid is identical
to that of the dolman.

The green breeches were
decorated with a flat braid
in the form of a Hungarian
knot at the opening of the
fall fly, and flat yellow braid
on the seam of the trousers.

The NCO's coat was of the same cut and
colour as the soldiers' ; it was decorated
with a green and gold aglet, of which there
is an example in the Musée de l'Empire. However, other drawings show scarlet and gold
aglets. With fashion, the skirts of the coat
got shorter and the turn-backs were cut
straight.
The waistcoat was decorated with green braid
mixed with gold; although it has not been
presented here, there exists a model with a
scarlet collar decorated with trimmings.

ARMAMENT and EQUIPMENT

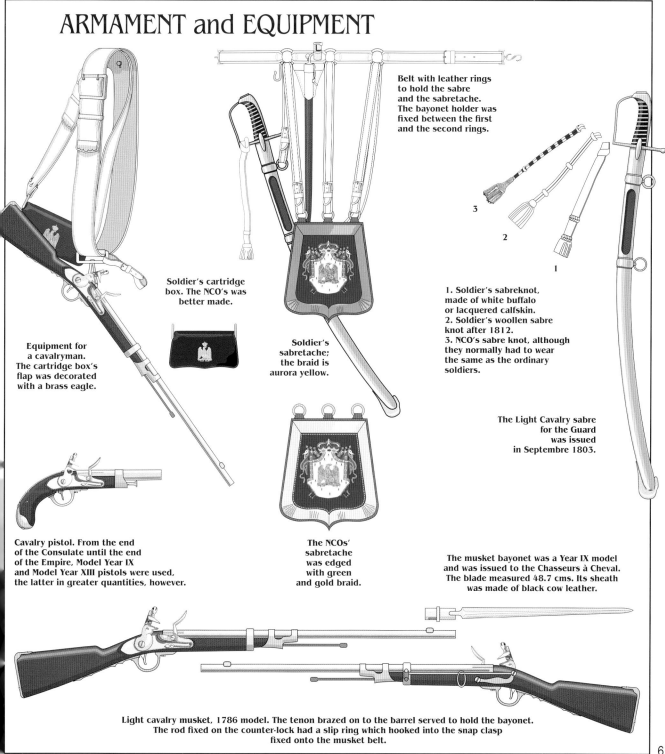

Belt with leather rings to hold the sabre and the sabretache. The bayonet holder was fixed between the first and the second rings.

Soldier's cartridge box. The NCO's was better made.

Equipment for a cavalryman. The cartridge box's flap was decorated with a brass eagle.

Soldier's sabretache; the braid is aurora yellow.

1. Soldier's sabreknot, made of white buffalo or lacquered calfskin.
2. Soldier's woollen sabre knot after 1812.
3. NCO's sabre knot, although they normally had to wear the same as the ordinary soldiers.

The Light Cavalry sabre for the Guard was issued in Septembre 1803.

Cavalry pistol. From the end of the Consulate until the end of the Empire, Model Year IX and Model Year XIII pistols were used, the latter in greater quantities, however.

The NCOs' sabretache was edged with green and gold braid.

The musket bayonet was a Year IX model and was issued to the Chasseurs à Cheval. The blade measured 48.7 cms. Its sheath was made of black cow leather.

Light cavalry musket, 1786 model. The tenon brazed on to the barrel served to hold the bayonet. The rod fixed on the counter-lock had a slip ring which hooked into the snap clasp fixed onto the musket belt.

SADDLES

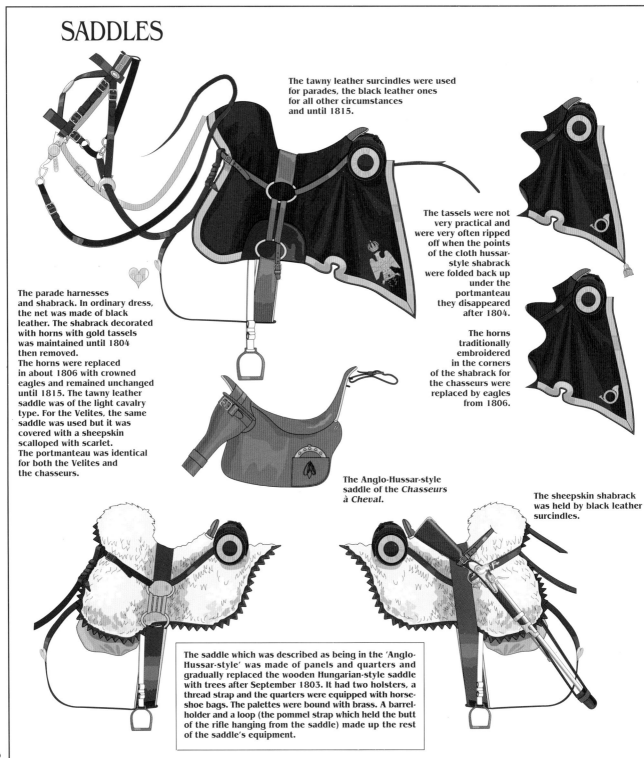

The tawny leather surcindles were used for parades, the black leather ones for all other circumstances and until 1815.

The tassels were not very practical and were very often ripped off when the points of the cloth hussar-style shabrack were folded back up under the portmanteau they disappeared after 1804.

The horns traditionally embroidered in the corners of the shabrack for the chasseurs were replaced by eagles from 1806.

The parade harnesses and shabrack. In ordinary dress, the net was made of black leather. The shabrack decorated with horns with gold tassels was maintained until 1804 then removed.
The horns were replaced in about 1806 with crowned eagles and remained unchanged until 1815. The tawny leather saddle was of the light cavalry type. For the Velites, the same saddle was used but it was covered with a sheepskin scalloped with scarlet.
The portmanteau was identical for both the Velites and the chasseurs.

The Anglo-Hussar-style saddle of the *Chasseurs à Cheval*.

The sheepskin shabrack was held by black leather surcindles.

The saddle which was described as being in the 'Anglo-Hussar-style' was made of panels and quarters and gradually replaced the wooden Hungarian-style saddle with trees after September 1803. It had two holsters, a thread strap and the quarters were equipped with horse-shoe bags. The palettes were bound with brass. A barrel-holder and a loop (the pommel strap which held the butt of the rifle hanging from the saddle) made up the rest of the saddle's equipment.

The NCOs

Maréchal-des-Logis-Chef in morning coat. The coat was basically used by these NCOs, who could decorate the items of their uniform (breeches and waistcoat for example) with nankeen braid and white thread trimmings according to the disposition of the uniform items.

As well as the rank and seniority stripes, the NCOs were more richly dressed than the soldiers. Thus the square braid, the flat embroidery and the trimmings, all the facings in fact, were made of wool mixed with one-third gold.

Likewise, braid and trimmings on the dolman and on the forage caps, like the loops and the braid of the cord on the forage cap, were made of scarlet wool laced with gold.

The trimming on the waistcoat and dolmans, and pelisse and breeches à la Hussarde were used more frequently for the NCOs.

The NCOs' aglet was theoretically scarlet and gold, although certain authors show it as yellow and gold. The hat had a gold braid cockade, the ribbon curls were green with a gold centre.

Maréchal-des-Logis in full dress. The NCOs did not use a musket and so did not have the straps to hold it nor the bayonet sheath on the belt.

Maréchal-des-Logis in town dress for Sundays.

Town dress with a coat. The NCO used embroidered breeches and nankeen waistcoat, all depending on his own financial ressources.

Maréchal-des-Logis in campaign dress.

TRUMPETER'S FULL DRESS

For full dress, the trumpeters used a silver trumpet decorated with a trumpet pennant, a leftover from Consular Guard days; only the mottoes changed. This pennant was considered as standard of the *Chasseurs* of the Guard.

It was presented in the collection of the Prince of the Moskova, decorated with a tricolour cravat. Its shape was identical to that of a cavalry pennant.

The trumpeter used a white fur colback for full dress and a shabrack decorated with a horn in each corner.

As all the other corps of cavalry of the Old Guard, the principal colour of the trumpeter's uniform was sky blue and crimson. The dolman's plaits were gold mixed with crimson; for the pelisse it was crimson with gold mixed with gold and sky blue; the woollen belt loops were also gold mixed with sky blue. The collar of the dolman was first sky blue then crimson.

The trumpeters wore gauntlets, one of their peculiarities when wearing full dress.

Detail of the trumpeter's pennant in the Chasseurs à Cheval at the beginning of the Empire. EF stands for *'Empire Français'* (the French Empire).

Trumpeter wearing ceremonial full dress at the beginning of the Empire, from the front.

Trumpeter wearing ceremonial full dress from 1804-1808.

MARCHING DRESS for TRUMPETERS

Trumpeter in full dress towards 1808-1811. The green pennant was replaced by a crimson one bearing the Imperial arms. Rigo explained on his plate No 179 in the *'le Plumet'* that a German source had represented a trumpeter with all-gold braid and stripes, probably an economy measure. However, the mixed facings were taken up again after 1813 in order to distinguish the Old Guard squadrons from the Young ones.

Trumpeter during the 1809 Campaign. There was no sabretache for the second uniform dress so the full dress one was protected by a waxed cloth sheath.

Trumpeter at Austerlitz, December 1805. He is using the sky blue campaign dress shabrack with braid. The full dress one was crimson and was left behind at the *dépôt*. The coat was rolled and worn over the shoulder with the purpose of protecting the torso during charges.

MARCHING DRESS for TRUMPETERS

Trumpeter during the Spanish Campaign. The trumpeters generally used the NCOs cartridge box, the side panels of the box being made of brass. This practice was not systematic, however.

Trumpeter wearing an 'à la Chasseur' coat. The Riding breeches were the same as those worn by the soldiers but the base colour was the trumpeter's celestial blue.

Trumpeter about 1812. It seems that it was perhaps during the Russian Campaign that the campaign marching dress sabretache with a leather flap decorated with a brass eagle appeared.

Trumpeter towards 1814. The grey riding breeches are those which were regularly issued to all the cavalrymen in the regiment.

TOWN and QUARTERS DRESS

Stable dress. This trumpeter has put on shoes in place of his boots and a pair of black gaiters from the Infantry of the Guard's campaign dress.

Trumpeter in Sunday town dress, according to the Alsatian Collections.

Trumpet-Major wearing the chasseur's coat. His rank was distinguishable by the two gold stripes on the facings. The collar, the facings and the lapels were usually decorated with three gold stripes.

Trumpet-Major wearing a frock-coat. One supposes that he was the only one among all the trumpeters in the regiment to use this item.

Trumpeter wearing summer town dress.

Brigadier-Trompette wearing winter town dress.

CLOTHING and EQUIPMENT

The bicorne had gold cords or gold mixed with celestial blue, influenced, of course, by fashion.

Shoulder trefoil made of flat crimson plaits edged with gold, or made in the same way as those of the braid on the edges of the dolman.

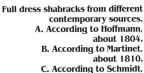

The marks of rank attributed to the trumpeters:
1. Trumpeter with one seniority stripe
2. *Brigadier-Trompette* having the rank of *Maréchal-des-Logis.*
3. Trumpet-Major with the rank of *Maréchal-des-Logis-Chef.*

Full dress shabracks from different contemporary sources.
A. According to Hoffmann, about 1804.
B. According to Martinet, about 1810.
C. According to Schmidt, about 1811.

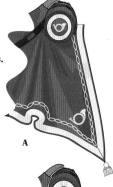

A

The position of the stripes on the waistcoat was the same as that of the NCOs.

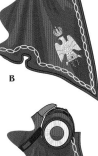

B

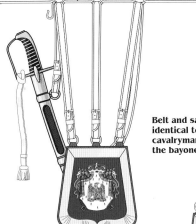

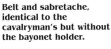

Belt and sabretache, identical to the cavalryman's but without the bayonet holder.

C

Trumpeter's '*à la Chasseur*' coat. During the Empire, fashion affected the trumpeter's coat as much as it did the soldier's. It was thus that the turn backs were sown up, the triangle formed at the bottom of the skirts eventually disappearing.

The sabretache was decorated with a gold stripe and a gold and celestial blue trimming, like on the regulation model seen on the left.
The sabretache above on the right was drawn by the German artist Boersch, around 1811.

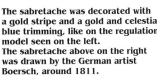

The Hungarian-style breeches were decorated with knots of the same origin with flat gold and crimson plaits, like the side seams.

The trumpeter had a light cavalry sabre for the Guard and a Year IX mle cavalry pistol.

The KETTLEDRUMMERS

Like Lucien Rousselot, Hoffmann represented the drummer as being very young.
Rigo however, on his plate No 8, tells us a little more about this person. His name was Jean-Bruneau Lemoine and was 18 in 1806.
He was *Brigadier-Trompette* with regimental headquarters and remained so until his tragic death during the Madrid riots, 2 May 1808. It can be presumed that at 18 or 19 he had reached adult size.
The uniform did not change after the Consular Guard except for the Imperial decorations.
The Eastern fashion which was in on their return from Egypt, reminds us that the *Chasseurs* were Bonaparte's scouts during this expedition. The Musée de l'Armée has in it possession a portrait of this kettledrummer wearing trumpeter's '*à la Hussarde*' dress of which it may be supposed that this was the kettledrummer's second dress.

It was on the top of the headstall that the horse's copper panache holder (one blue, one white, one scarlet and one green) was fitted. The parade bridle was made of black varnished leather.
The nose-piece was fitted with a martingale connected to the chest preventing the horse from lifting its head.
The saddle was Turkish-style covered with a Hungarian-style saddle cloth very amply covered with gold braid. First of all it was green - the colour of the *Chasseurs à Cheval* - then crimson (see the following plate).
Two rings fixed to the large crescent-shaped saddle pommel served to hold the timpani in place with leather thongs which were passed under the steel counterhoop, itself held to the body of the kettledrum by means of eight lugs.

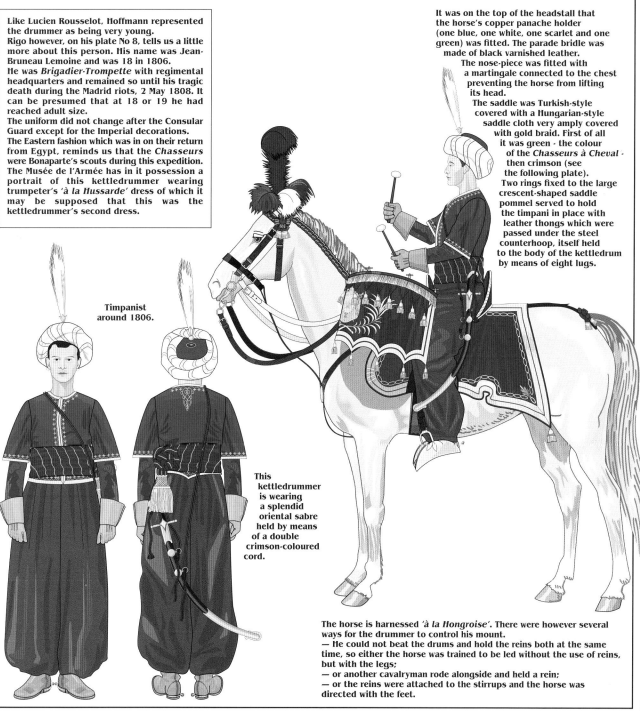

Timpanist around 1806.

This kettledrummer is wearing a splendid oriental sabre held by means of a double crimson-coloured cord.

The horse is harnessed '*à la Hongroise*'. There were however several ways for the drummer to control his mount.
— He could not beat the drums and hold the reins both at the same time, so either the horse was trained to be led without the use of reins, but with the legs;
— or another cavalryman rode alongside and held a rein;
— or the reins were attached to the stirrups and the horse was directed with the feet.

The KETTLEDRUMMERS

The kettledrummer after 1810 and his *yalek* (Arabian horsemen's waistcoat) was portrayed by Bœrsch, mounted, and on the right, seen from the rear. The item of clothing worn under the yalek was called a *'béniche'* was also gold braided. The silk belt was also called a *'hezam'*.

After 1808, according to Bœrsch and Schmidt, the kettledrummer continued to be dressed Oriental-style. The shabrack was simplified and the drum aprons bore Imperial livery and crowned eagles.
The one in green was drawn by Bœrsch and the blue one by Schmidt. However, the celestial blue background colour corresponds to the general appearance of the uniforms worn by musicians of the Guard. The one in green must very certainly be considered as fictitious.
It is however difficult - with the lack of incontestable, and unchallenged, sources - to say that one is more 'correct' than the other.
That is why both versions are presented here in the same way as Rigo did in his plate No 195.

According to the two German artists, the difference between the two also concerned the turban, called a *'schal'*.
For Bœrsch, the schal was white with green stripes; whereas for Schmidt, it was white with gold stripes.
The kettledrummers in both cases do not have weapons of any kind.

A timpanist after 1810 wearing his blue yalek, drawn by Schmidt. The *'charoual'* (the trousers) were in both cases crimson.

Timpanist in full dress about 1811. Note the change in the decoration of the kettledrum apron which has lost all its oriental motifs, replaced by the less exotic, but more impressive ones of the Imperial livery.

70

OFFICER'S FULL DRESS

The officers of the *Chasseurs à Cheval* of the Guard's full dress did not really change very much during the course of the Empire.
There were certainly a few differences in the trimmings of the dolmans and the pelisses; however the contemporary artistic reference is still the portrait of Lieutenant Dieudonné by Géricault.
The sabres of the officers in the Chasseurs were very rich and the factory at Versailles was the principal supplier of such weapons.
For more information on this subject it is suggested that Michel Pétard's study on arms and equipment be consulted.
The officer in this plate has been given a Year XIII model light cavalry sabre.

Junior officer - lieutenants and captains were thought to be junior officers - wearing full dress towards 1808.

On parade, the officer used a natural panther skin shabrack. The head was placed on th rear part of the saddle. The tail therefore was at the front and hung to the left as a general rule. The stirrup leathers were made of red morocco and the stirrups were etched and gold-leafed. The harness included golden buckles and a series of gilded brass decorations just like the plate on the front and the chest pieces.

FULL DRESS and MARCHING DRESS

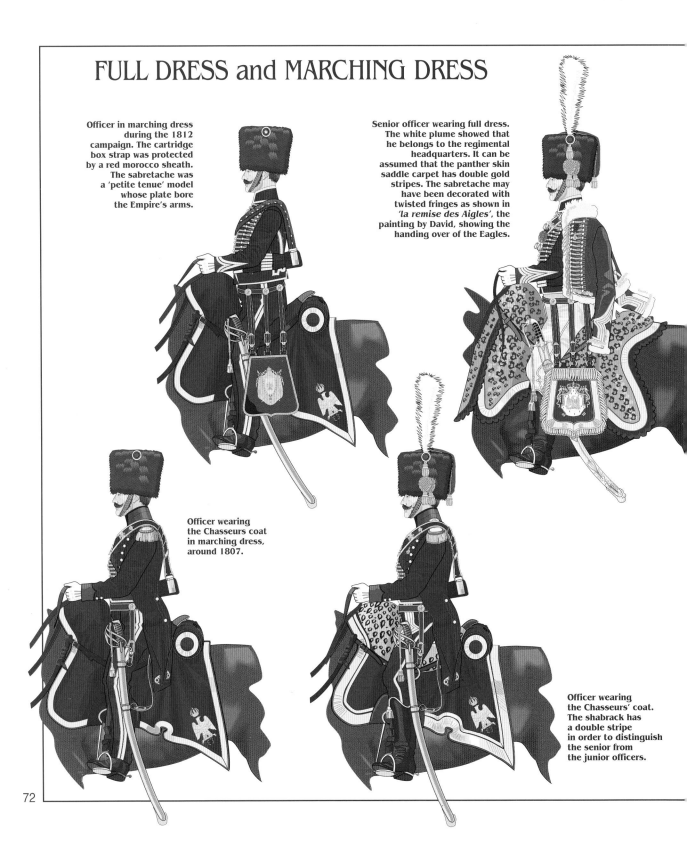

Officer in marching dress during the 1812 campaign. The cartridge box strap was protected by a red morocco sheath. The sabretache was a 'petite tenue' model whose plate bore the Empire's arms.

Senior officer wearing full dress. The white plume showed that he belongs to the regimental headquarters. It can be assumed that the panther skin saddle carpet has double gold stripes. The sabretache may have been decorated with twisted fringes as shown in *'la remise des Aigles'*, the painting by David, showing the handing over of the Eagles.

Officer wearing the Chasseurs coat in marching dress, around 1807.

Officer wearing the Chasseurs' coat. The shabrack has a double stripe in order to distinguish the senior from the junior officers.

72

TOWN DRESS

Officer of the Emperor's suite during the 1809 campaign.
The red plume has been proposed by Colonel Lefebvre-Desnouette taken from a painting showing the Imperial suite on the bridge of boats on Lobau Island.

Officer wearing summer town dress. As with the preceding and the following drawings, this officer is wearing a splendid pair of coloured leather boots. His Hungarian-style breeches and his dolman are covered with very richly decorated embroidery.

Officer in 'à la chasseur' going out dress. This dress is incredibly modest compared with the dress worn by the officer in the centre, but the material from which it was tailored was nonetheless more delicate than the soldiers'.

Officer wearing a morning frock coat.

Regimental Doctor (Major). This picture has been realised from a period miniature. He is wearing officer's dress without having the right to wear it, as he has no marks of rank. He does however have the emblems of the health corps: acanthus leaves and crimson velvet.

Officer in Social dress.

CLOTHING

Using the descriptions Michel Pétard made of the ranks in the chapter entitled *'L'officier de Chasseur à Cheval'* (in the book *'La Cavalerie légère du 1er Empire'* - the Light Cavalry of the First Empire), and both the plates by Rigo in *'le Plumet'* and those by Lucien Rousselot, an attempt has been made to classify the ranks of the officers in this corps.

In the *'à la Chasseur'* dress there were epaulettes on the coat and stripes on the trousers, and braid on the sleeves of the pelisse and the dolman. Because of the well-entrenched traditions in the Guards regiments where the distinction between officers and their opposite numbers in the units of the Line was concerned, it is very quickly clear that certain liberties have been taken, liberties which make a logical explanation of this distinction - if the regulations are to be respected - all the more complicated.

One can imagine that this Second-Lieutenant is wearing a contra-epaulette like the one on Plate No 70 by Lucien Rousselot.

1   2   3

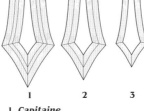

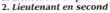

1   2   3

1. *Capitaine*
2. *Lieutenant en premier*
2. *Lieutenant en second*

Social dress and town dress bicorne.

Squadron Commander with a braid twist epaulette on the right.

Waistcoat.

With the changes of fashion, the turn backs were sown on to the skirts which eventually led to the disappearance of the turn back.

When the list of the officers in the corps is consulted, it seems that the rank of *'colonel en second'* is missing; this was the equivalent of a Brigadier.

Colonel with two braid twist epaulettes.

Two 'braid twist epaulettes with three stars.

Colonel-Major, commanding the *Chasseur à Cheval* of the Guard Corps, who had Major-General rank according to Plate No 26 in *'le Plumet'*, which shows Lefebvre-Desnouette in 1808.

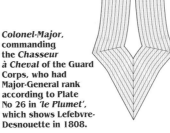

'A la Chasseur' coat. It was tailored like that of the soldiers, but the cloth was finer with a gold aglet. The horns were gold and placed on a crimson background colour.

Hungarian-style breeches with the position of the stripes of rank.

STANDARD-BEARERS

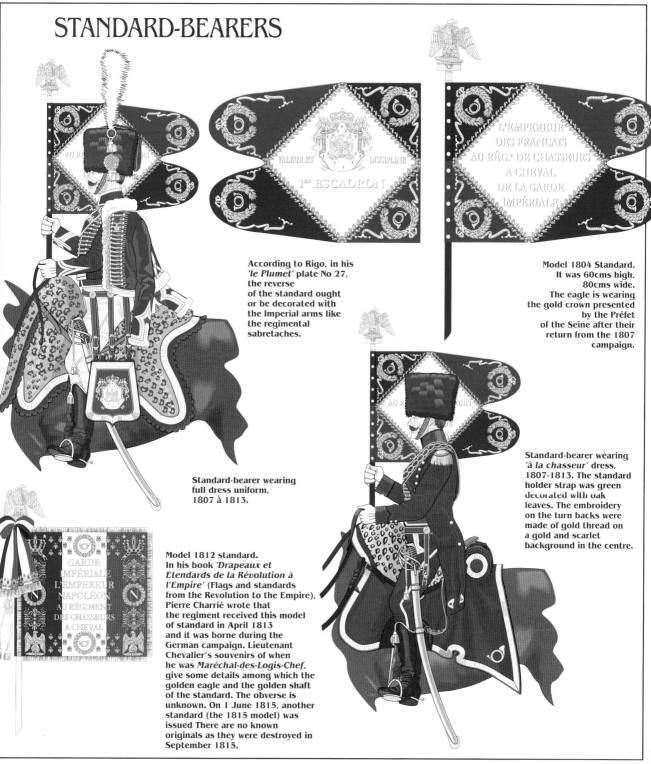

According to Rigo, in his *'le Plumet'* plate No 27, the reverse of the standard ought or be decorated with the Imperial arms like the regimental sabretaches.

Standard-bearer wearing full dress uniform, 1807 à 1813.

Model 1804 Standard. It was 60cms high, 80cms wide. The eagle is wearing the gold crown presented by the Préfet of the Seine after their return from the 1807 campaign.

Standard-bearer wearing *'à la chasseur'* dress, 1807-1813. The standard holder strap was green decorated with oak leaves. The embroidery on the turn backs were made of gold thread on a gold and scarlet background in the centre.

Model 1812 standard. In his book *'Drapeaux et Etendards de la Révolution à l'Empire'* (Flags and standards from the Revolution to the Empire), Pierre Charrié wrote that the regiment received this model of standard in April 1813 and it was borne during the German campaign. Lieutenant Chevalier's souvenirs of when he was *Maréchal-des-Logis-Chef*, give some details among which the golden eagle and the golden shaft of the standard. The obverse is unknown. On 1 June 1815, another standard (the 1815 model) was issued There are no known originals as they were destroyed in September 1815.

The SECOND REGIMENT
of the CHASSEURS A CHEVAL
and the Squadrons of the Young Guard

When he returned from Russia, the Emperor created four new two-company squadrons (the eleventh to the eighteenth) in the *Chasseurs à Cheval*.

The squadrons of the so-called 'Young Guard'

In 1813 and 1814, the 6th, 7th , 8th and 9th squadrons, called the Young Guard took part in the German Campaign and they fought especially in France alongside their elders and the cavalrymen of the three regiments of scouts. During the Restoration, with the cuts in numbers which were planned as the *Corps Royal des Chasseurs de France* was being formed, these cavalrymen deserted en masse, or were transferred to the regiments of cavalry of the Line, havens and regiments which they did not hesitate to give up when Napoleon came back from exile and recreated the Cavalry of the Guard.

The 2nd Regiment

As Napoleon had intended to reinforce the cavalry of the Guard considerably, he decided on 15 May 1815 to create a new regiment of light cavalry called first of all *'Tirailleurs de la Garde'* then *'Hussards Eclaireurs de la Jeune Garde'* (the Hussar-Scouts of the Young Guard)

The administration of the regiment was obviously given over to the administrative of the *Chasseurs à Cheval* of the Guard.

On 26 May, having almost got back up to strength again, the ephemeral *'Hussars of the Guard'* were finally given the name of *2nd regiment of Chasseurs à Cheval of the Guard*. Lieutenant-General Lefebvre-Desnouettes, who was a weapon inspector for the light cavalry of the Guard was above all a Colonel in the *Chasseurs à Cheval* of the Old Guard ; so he became the colonel of the new regiment, leaving *Maréchal de Camp* Marlin-de-Douai to take command of the regiment with the rank of *Major* (in the Old Guard).

Having replaced the 1st Regiment of *Chasseurs à Cheval* of the Guard in Paris, the regiment did not take part in the Belgian Campaign and was not present for the disaster at Waterloo. Their loyalty to the Emperor caused them numerous problems with the King's partisans in the first days of the summer of 1815.

There followed progressive lay-offs in the provinces from September to November 1815 from Saumur to Bourges. The cavalrymen who were still present in spite of a spate of desertions made up the basic structure for the four new squadrons of Hussars of the new Royal cavalry.

Recruitment

The cavalrymen in the regiment came mainly from the oldest regiments in the Guard (*Chasseurs à Cheval*, Dragoons, Grenadiers and Lancers) or from the regiments of the Line which had to hand over cavalrymen with four years' service or campaigning. The cavalrymen coming from the Line were mainly former Chasseurs in the Young Guard squadrons who had been sent to these same regiments of the Line a year previously.

This was the rather torturous path which Captain Parquin, the famous memorialist, followed after 1813, the year when he was a *Lieutenant* of the 11th Company of the Young Guard before being promoted to Captain of Cuirassiers in 1814. He returned to the 2nd Regiment of the *Chasseurs à Cheval* of the Guard in 1815.

REGIMENTAL STRENGTH.

A few days after its incorporation, the 2nd Regiment of *Chasseurs à Cheval* of the Guards numbered twenty-seven officers for seven hundred and nine cavalrymen with its four squadrons and headquarters.

At the time when the *Chasseurs à Cheval* of the Old Guard were fighting at Waterloo, the regiment numbered 53 officers for 921 cavalrymen. In July there were only 35 officers and 640 Chasseurs and NCOs. When it was finally disbanded the regimental rolls listed 40 officers and 266 cavalrymen only.

The SQUADRONS of the YOUNG GUARD

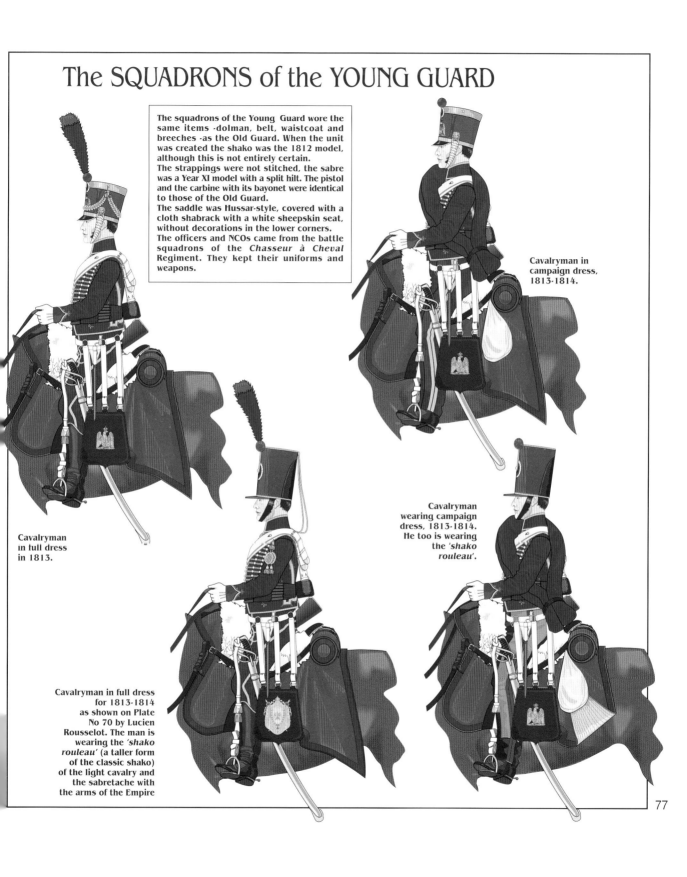

The squadrons of the Young Guard wore the same items -dolman, belt, waistcoat and breeches -as the Old Guard. When the unit was created the shako was the 1812 model, although this is not entirely certain.

The strappings were not stitched, the sabre was a Year XI model with a split hilt. The pistol and the carbine with its bayonet were identical to those of the Old Guard.

The saddle was Hussar-style, covered with a cloth shabrack with a white sheepskin seat, without decorations in the lower corners.

The officers and NCOs came from the battle squadrons of the *Chasseur à Cheval* Regiment. They kept their uniforms and weapons.

Cavalryman in campaign dress, 1813-1814.

Cavalryman in full dress in 1813.

Cavalryman wearing campaign dress, 1813-1814. He too is wearing the 'shako rouleau'.

Cavalryman in full dress for 1813-1814 as shown on Plate No 70 by Lucien Rousselot. The man is wearing the 'shako rouleau' (a taller form of the classic shako) of the light cavalry and the sabretache with the arms of the Empire

The 2nd RÉGIMENT of CHASSEURS A CHEVAL

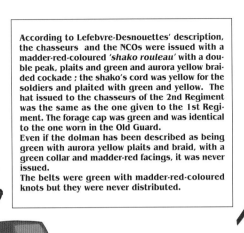

According to Lefebvre-Desnouettes' description, the chasseurs and the NCOs were issued with a madder-red-coloured *'shako rouleau'* with a double peak, plaits and green and aurora yellow braided cockade ; the shako's cord was yellow for the soldiers and plaited with green and yellow. The hat issued to the chasseurs of the 2nd Regiment was the same as the one given to the 1st Regiment. The forage cap was green and was identical to the one worn in the Old Guard.

Even if the dolman has been described as being green with aurora yellow plaits and braid, with a green collar and madder-red facings, it was never issued.

The belts were green with madder-red-coloured knots but they were never distributed.

Cavalryman in full dress in 1815 according to Commandant Bucquoy 's set of cards and the description made by Lefebvre-Desnouettes on 27 May 1815. The regiment was created on 21 May 1815.

The pelisse was theoretically madder-red with yellow plaits and braid.
The fur was black. It seems though that the pelisses destined for the Old Guard were given to the 2nd Regiment instead.
The Hungarian-style breeches were not planned.
The riding breeches were green with two madder-red stripes. In fact, trousers with only one stripe were the only ones worn.

Cavalryman wearing campaign dress in 1815 according to the record of supplies distributed to the regiment in the second quarter of 1815. Note that there are no dolmans, no Hungarian breeches, nor cord to fasten the shakos with. On the other hand, the larger equipment and the weapons are all there.

Cavalryman wearing campaign dress (left).

Maréchal-des-logis (right) in 1815. He seems to have kept the pelisse which he wore when he served in the Old Guard squadrons.

The TRUMPETERS

Trumpeter in the squadrons of the Young Guard wearing campaign dress, 1813-1814. It seems that the trumpeter has kept his pelisse and his colback from his time in the Old Guard.

Trumpeter in the 2nd Regiment of the *Chasseurs à Cheval* of the Young Guard wearing marching dress in 1815.

Trumpet-Major in 1815. Described by Boissellier, this trumpeter, seeing his seniority, has obviously come from the squadrons of the Old Guard whose dolman and sabre he is still wearing. The shako is perhaps that of an NCO. Nonetheless, according to the records of supplies there was only one dolman issue to the trumpet-major of the regiment and it was sky-blue with scarlet plaits.

Trumpeter in the 2nd Regiment of *Chasseurs à Cheval* of the Young Guard wearing campaign dress in 1815, according to the old archives of the Ministry of Defence. The yellow strappings seem a bit strange but the period did not lend itself particularly well to the strict application of all the rules concerning dress and so anything is possible. Here again this trumpeter seems to have come from one of the squadrons of the Old Guard, seeing as he is wearing the sabre and the dolman.

This Trumpet-Major in 1815 is wearing a marvellous jacket. This drawing has been taken from a study by Boisselier.

The OFFICERS

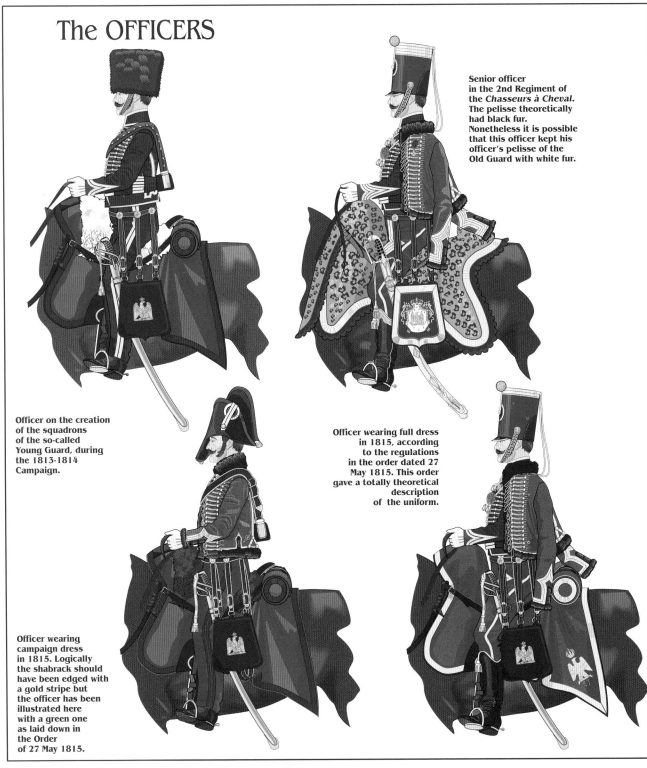

Senior officer
in the 2nd Regiment of
the *Chasseurs à Cheval*.
The pelisse theoretically
had black fur.
Nonetheless it is possible
that this officer kept his
officer's pelisse of the
Old Guard with white fur.

Officer on the creation
of the squadrons
of the so-called
Young Guard, during
the 1813-1814
Campaign.

Officer wearing full dress
in 1815, according
to the regulations
in the order dated 27
May 1815. This order
gave a totally theoretical
description
of the uniform.

Officer wearing
campaign dress
in 1815. Logically
the shabrack should
have been edged with
a gold stripe but
the officer has been
illustrated here
with a green one
as laid down in
the Order
of 27 May 1815.

OFFICERS, SOLDIERS and TRUMPETERS

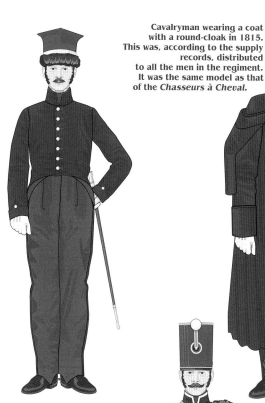

Cavalryman wearing a coat with a round-cloak in 1815. This was, according to the supply records, distributed to all the men in the regiment. It was the same model as that of the *Chasseurs à Cheval*.

Officer in 1815 wearing a dolman and riding breeches. Unlike a lot of soldiers, the officers wore a cord going from their chests to the shako so that the rider did not lose it.

Officer in 1815. Officers wore a frock coat for morning dress without aglets as usual in the Guard.

Officer in quarters dress, 1815. The coat is jacket-like and the hat a Polish-style forage cap.

Trumpeter, according to the Alsatian Collections. The pelisse, the dolman and the trumpet cord seem unrealistic. The lack of sabretache however, is plausible In so far as the regiment was not completely equipped.

All officers had a shako with a peak and a leather reinforcement behind it. Three double braids of gold plaits, a gold pompom and a gold cord made up the head-dress. The tassels on the cord indicated the rank. If the hat was identical in shape to that of the soldiers, the forage cap was Polish-style, Astrakhan fur-lined. The top of the hat was madder-red-coloured.
The dolman, the pelisse and the belt were identical for the senior officers to those of their opposite numbers in the Old Guard
Junior officers had a green dolman, plaited with gold with madder-red collar and facings. The buttons were yellow and Hussar-style. The pelisse was of a madder-red colour described as light with gold plaits and stripes. The fur was black Astrakhan. The belt was made of green and madder-red-coloured plaits, with gold beads.

BIBLIOGRAPHY

— **L'ARMÉE FRANÇAISE.** *Lucien Rousselot*

Planche n°	**13.**	Les dragons de la garde impériale
Planche n°	**23.**	Les grenadiers à cheval
Planche n°	**45.**	Les grenadiers à cheval
Planches n° 47, 65, 75.		Les chevau-légers lanciers polonais
Planche n°	**53.**	Les dragons
Planches n° 69, 70, 83, 94.		Les chasseurs à cheval

— **LE PLUMET.** *Rigo*

Planche n°	**5.**	Timbalier des Grenadiers
Planche n°	**7.**	Timbalier des Dragons
Planche n°	**8.**	Timbaliers des Chasseurs à cheval
Planche n°	**21.**	Porte-étendard des grenadiers
Planche n°	**22.**	Porte-étendard des dragons
Planche n°	**27.**	Porte-étendard des chasseurs à cheval
Planche n°	**32.**	Porte-étendard des mameluks
Planche n°	**36.**	Porte-étendard des chevau légers lanciers
Planche n°	**179.**	Chasseurs à cheval trompette
Planche n°	**195.**	Timbaliers des Chasseurs à cheval
Planche n°	**207.**	Guidon des dragons
Planche n°	**217.**	Trompette des dragons

— **UNIFORMES** (*French magazine*)

Uniformes n° **52.** Le grenadier à cheval de la Garde. *Michel Pétard*
Uniformes n° **57.** Le dragon de la Garde. *Michel Pétard*
Uniformes n° **77.** Le lancier polonais de la Garde. *Michel Pétard*
Uniformes n° **88.** Le tirailleur-grenadier. *Lucien Rousselot*

BOOKS

— **Napoléon's Army print of Martinet.** G. Dempsey
— **Uniformes des armées de Waterloo.** U. Perricoli. *Editions Vilo*
— **Equipement militaire, la Garde Impériale. Tome V.** M. Pétard
— **Napoléon's soldiers.** G. Dempsey. *Arms and Armour Press*
— **Les polonais de Napoléon.** J. Tranié et J.-C. Carmigniani. *Copernic*
— **Guide des uniformes de l'Armée Française 1780-1848.** H. Malibran
— **Napoléon's elite cavalry.** E. Ryan, illust. L. Rousselot. *Greenhill Books*
— **L'épopée napoléonienne.** F.-G. Hourtoulle, illust. J. Girbal. *Histoire & Collections*
— **La cavalerie au temps des chevaux.** Colonel Dugué Mac Carthy. *EPA*
— **Napoleonic uniforms.** J. R. Elting et R. Knötel. *Mac Millan*
— **La Garde Impériale.** L. Fallou, illust. Grammont
— **Le 2e Régiment de Chasseurs à Cheval de la Garde.** O. Lapray

ACKNOWLEDGMENTS

We should like to thank *Rigo*, *Michel Pétard*, Dr. *François-Guy Hourtoulle* and *Jean-Louis Viau* for their precious help, both morally and editing-wise. We pay tribute once again where it is due, to them.

We should also like to thank Mr *Lapray* for his invaluable help and his work on the Chasseurs à Cheval of the Young Guard Squadrons and the 2nd Regiment.

Design and lay-out by André Jouineau and Jean-Marie Mongin, © *Histoire & Collections* 2003
Computer drawings by André Jouineau

histoire & collections
SA au capital de 182 938,82 €

5, avenue de la République
F-75541 Paris Cédex 11
Téléphone : 01 40 21 18 20
Fax : 01 47 00 51 11

This book has been designed, typed, laid-out and processed by *Histoire & Collections* fully on integrated computer equipment

Printed by Zure
Spain, European Union
January 2003